See How They Grow

See How Rabbits Grow

Kathryn Walker

PowerKiDS
press™

New York

Published in 2009 by The Rosen Publishing Group Inc.
29 East 21st Street, New York, NY 10010

First Edition

Library of Congress Cataloging-in-Publication Data

Walker, Kathryn, 1957-
  See how rabbits grow / Kathryn Walker. — 1st ed.
      p. cm. — (See how they grow)
  Includes index.
  ISBN 978-1-4358-2831-5 (library binding)
  ISBN 978-1-4358-2879-7 (paperback)
  ISBN 978-1-4358-2880-3 (6-pack)
  1. Rabbits—Development—Juvenile literature. I. Title.
  QL737.L32W36 2009
  636.932'2—dc22

                          2008027165

Manufactured in China

The publishers would like to thank the following for allowing us to reproduce
their pictures in this book:
Getty images: cover (Martin Ruegner /Image Bank), title page and 19 (GK Hart/Vikki Hart
/Image Bank), 11 (Steve Shott/Dorling Kindersley collection), 17 (Gary Randall/Taxi), 18
(Catherine Ledner/Stone), 22 (Wendy Ashton/Taxi). Discovery Picture Library: 9, 23. FLPA:
4 (David Hosking), 5 (Gerard Lacz), 6 (Cyril Ruoso/JH Editorial/Minden Pictures), 7 (Edwin
Giesbers/ Foto Natura), 8 (Foto Natura), 13 (Andrew Parkinson), 14 (Nigel Cattlin), 15
(Gerard Lacz), 20 and 21 (Mike Lane). Istockphoto: 10, 12 (Barbara Henry), 16 (Nico Smith).

Web Sites

Due to the changing nature of Internet links, PowerKids Press has
developed an online list of Web sites related to the subject of this book.
This site is updated regularly. Please use this link to access this list:
www.powerkidslinks.com/shtg/rabbit

Contents

What is a rabbit?

Rabbits are found in many parts of the world. Wild rabbits live in woods, grasslands, and sand dunes. They are like **domestic rabbits** in many ways. Domestic rabbits are ones that people keep as pets.

▼ Strong back legs and feet help a rabbit to move quickly.

Rabbits have very good hearing. Their eyes can see in almost all directions. Their twitching noses quickly pick up new smells. Rabbits are always looking out for signs of danger. Many animals kill rabbits for food.

▲ A rabbit's large ears can turn in any direction to pick up a noise.

Wild rabbits

Most types of wild rabbits live in large groups. They live together in **warrens**. A warren is a set of underground holes, or **burrows**. Narrow tunnels link these burrows together.

▼ Rabbits shelter inside their warrens.

Rabbits sleep in their burrows for most of the day. They leave their burrows to find food. They usually do this in the evening and early morning.

▲ These rabbits are keeping watch at an entrance to their warren. Each warren has several entrances.

Domestic rabbits

More than 2,000 years ago, the ancient Romans farmed rabbits for meat and fur. Today, lots of people keep rabbits as pets. Rabbits enjoy the company of people.

▲ Rabbits often get along well with other family pets, such as guinea pigs.

Rabbit Fact

You can train a rabbit to use a litter tray. This is important if the rabbit is kept indoors.

Regular brushing helps to keep a pet rabbit clean and healthy.

A rabbit is born

A mother rabbit can have between four and twelve babies at a time. Rabbit babies are called **kittens** or kits. The mother prepares a cosy nest for her kittens. She pulls fur from her own body to make this nest.

▼ Kittens' eyes stay shut for the first few weeks of their lives.

The kittens are born without fur. At first, they cannot hear or see. The mother visits her nest once or twice a day. Then the kittens can feed on her milk.

▶ The mother's milk gives her kittens all the food they need for the first few weeks.

Growing up

At three weeks, the kittens' eyes are open and they have thick fur coats. They begin to eat solid food. Rabbits finish growing when they are between six and eight months old. Female rabbits are called **does** and males are called **bucks**.

▲ Kittens huddle together when they are tired. This helps them stay warm.

Rabbit Fact

Pet rabbits can live for eight to twelve years. Many wild rabbits die in their first year.

▼ Young rabbits like to explore, but they stay close together for safety.

What rabbits eat

Rabbits eat only plants. Wild rabbits eat grasses, roots, and berries. Pet rabbits need vegetables, fruit, and hay. They should also have special rabbit food from a pet shop.

▼ Rabbits like to eat crops, such as the barley in this field. This is why farmers see them as pests.

▼ Rabbits like to gnaw on wood. This stops their teeth from growing too long.

All kinds of rabbits

There are many different types of rabbit.
The type that you see in the wild are
usually a grayish-brown color.

Rabbit Fact

Hares are members
of the rabbit family.
Hares are bigger than
rabbits. They have
longer legs and ears.

◀ Unlike rabbits,
most hares prefer
to live alone.

16

Pet rabbits come in all sizes and colors. There are special types called **breeds**. Some breeds have long hair. Some have long, floppy ears. These are called lop-eared rabbits.

Lop-eared rabbits look cute, but they cannot hear as well as other rabbits.

Choosing a pet rabbit

You need to choose a pet rabbit carefully. Some types grow to be large and will need big **hutches**. Long-haired rabbits need lots of brushing to stop their coats from getting tangled.

◄ This breed of rabbit is called the English Lop. These rabbits can weigh more than 11 lbs. (5 kg). All rabbits must be picked up very carefully, as this boy is doing.

▼ Pet rabbits are happier when they have company.

Rabbit Fact

Most rabbits do not like being picked up. They need to be handled gently, since they can easily be injured.

Pet rabbits like to have a companion. It is best to have two female or two male rabbits from the same **litter**.

Making a home

A pet rabbit needs a hutch with two parts. The main part should have a screen door. This is the living space. The other part should have a solid wooden door and **straw** inside. This is where the rabbit sleeps.

A rabbit hutch needs to be cleaned out every day.

A rabbit needs to run around outside its hutch. A long wire cage in the garden is the best place. This is called a **run**.

▼ A rabbit can eat fresh grass and wander around safely in a run.

Caring for a rabbit

A pet rabbit will need regular food and plenty of hay to eat. You need to clean out its hutch every day and make sure it gets plenty of exercise.

Playing helps a rabbit to stay fit and happy. Boxes, balls, and tubes all make great toys.

▼ Rabbits can make great pets if they are carefully looked after.

Big tubes like this can be play tunnels. They are a bit like a burrow and make good places to rest.

Glossary and Further Information

bedding Material used to make a comfortable place for a rabbit to sit or sleep. It may be a mixture of newspaper and wood shavings, straw, and hay.

breed A special type of rabbit.

buck A male rabbit.

burrow A hole in the ground made by a rabbit. It is used as a place to shelter.

doe A female rabbit.

domestic rabbit A rabbit that is kept as a pet.

hay Cut and dried grass used as food for some animals, such as rabbits.

hutch A cage for small animals, such as rabbits. A rabbit hutch is usually made of wood and wire screen.

kitten A baby rabbit.

litter The offspring, or young, born to an animal at one time.

litter tray A tray that an animal uses as its toilet.

run A long cage that protects rabbits as they wander around outdoors.

straw Dried stems of plants such as wheat or barley. It is used for animals to sleep on.

warren A set of underground holes and connecting tunnels where rabbits live.

Books

A Pet's Life: Rabbits
by Anita Ganeri
(Heinemann, 2003)

Caring For Your Rabbit
by Jill Foran (Weigl
Educational Publishers, 2003)

Index

Betty Crocker's

Cook It Quick

Betty Crocker's
Cook It Quick

Homemade Made Easy in 30 Minutes or Less

Hungry Minds™

NEW YORK, NY • CLEVELAND, OH • INDIANAPOLIS, IN

Hungry
Minds™

Published by
Hungry Minds, Inc.
909 Third Avenue
New York, NY 10022
www.hungryminds.com

For general information on Hungry Minds' products and services please contact our Customer Care Department within the U.S. at 800-762-2974, outside the U.S. at 317-572-3993 or fax 317-572-4002.

For sales inquiries and reseller information, including discounts, premium and bulk quantity sales, and foreign-language translations, please contact our Customer Care Department at 800-434-3422, fax 317-572-4002, or write to Hungry Minds, Inc., Attn: Customer Care Department, 10475 Crosspoint Boulevard, Indianapolis, IN 46256.

Library of Congress Cataloging-in-Publication Data

Crocker, Betty.
    Betty Crocker's cook it quick.
       p. cm.
    "Originally published as Betty Crocker's expressipes"—Copyr. p.
    Includes index.
    ISBN 0-7645-6424-2
    1. Quick and easy cookery. I. Crocker, Betty. Betty Crocker's expressipes.

    TX833.5 .C685 2001
    641.5'55—dc21   2001024140

General Mills, Inc.
Betty Crocker Kitchens
Manager, Publishing: Lois L. Tlusty
Recipe Development: Betty Crocker Kitchens Home Economists
Food Stylists: Betty Crocker Kitchens Food Stylists

Photographic Services
Photography: Photographic Services Department

Hungry Minds, Inc.
COVER AND BOOK DESIGN BY MICHELE LASEAU
JUNIOR DESIGNER HOLLY WITTENBERG

For consistent baking results, the Betty Crocker Kitchens recommend Gold Medal Flour.

For more great ideas visit **www.bettycrocker.com**

Manufactured in the United States of America
10 9 8 7 6 5 4 3 2 1

Cover Photos: Italian Burgers (page 75), Spicy Noodle Soup (page 43), and Raspberry-Chocolate Cream (page 169)
Originally published as *Betty Crocker's EXPRESSipes*

To All Busy People,

Come beat the clock with me! With these 100 quick recipes, you can have a home-cooked meal every night of the week, no matter how busy your day may be. In 30 minutes—or less—these delicious recipes can be ready and on the table.

Everyone in the family will find something they love. Kid favorites such as Easy Macaroni and Cheese, Chili Dog Wraps and Taco Joes are here, as well as elegant and appealing ideas such as Fresh Mushroom Fettuccine, Grilled Lime Chicken Breast and Lemony Seafood Risotto. From hurry-up post-game meals to entertaining, these recipes cover all the bases.

Want to go straight to the top ten hits for quick recipes? Turn to the first chapter, "10 Recipes You Can't Live Without" for great food in minutes. Looking for meatless meals? We've put 🔖 by every meatless recipe.

Together we can turn dinner into a relaxing—and tasty—time with family or friends. So tonight, why not try one of these easy-going recipes and enjoy the fun of a real home-cooked meal.

Betty Crocker

P.S. Check out the "Fix-It-Faster" tips at the beginning of every chapter.

Contents

Chapter 4

Quick Meaty Main Dishes

 meatless

Chapter 7

On the Side

Chapter 8

Simply Delicious Desserts

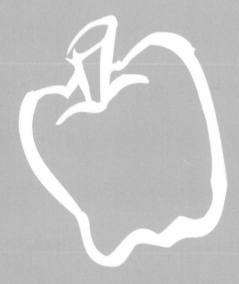

Chapter 1

10 Quick Recipes
You Can't Live Without!

meatless

Mini Meat Loaves
You Can't Live Without!

4 servings

1 *pound lean ground beef*

1/2 *cup dry bread crumbs*

1/4 *cup milk*

1/2 *teaspoon salt*

1/2 *teaspoon Worcestershire sauce, if desired*

1/4 *teaspoon pepper*

1 *small onion, finely chopped*

1 *egg*

1. Heat oven to 400°.

2. Mix all ingredients. Pat mixture in rectangle, 9 × 3 inches, in ungreased rectangular baking dish. Cut into 1 1/2-inch squares; separate squares slightly.

3. Bake uncovered about 25 minutes or until brown and until no longer pink in center and juice is clear.

1 Serving: Calories 305; Fat 18g; Cholesterol 120mg; Sodium 460mg; Carbohydrate 12g (Dietary Fiber 1g); Protein 25g

Easy Meatballs: This recipe can also be used for meatballs. Shape and cut meat mixture as directed above except shape into balls. Cook meatballs in 10-inch skillet over medium heat about 20 minutes, turning occasionally, until no longer pink in center and juice is clear.

12

Homemade Chicken Soup
You Can't Live Without!

4 servings

1 pound boneless, skinless
   chicken breast halves,
   cut into 1-inch pieces

1/4 cup all-purpose flour

1 tablespoon vegetable oil

1 medium onion, chopped
   (1/2 cup)

1/4 teaspoon garlic powder

1 can (49 1/2 ounces) ready-to-
   serve chicken broth

1 cup baby-cut carrots

1 tablespoon chopped fresh
   parsley, if desired

1 teaspoon dried thyme leaves

2 medium stalks celery, sliced

1 cup uncooked farfalle
   (bow-tie) pasta or wide
   noodles (2 ounces)

1. Toss chicken with flour. Heat oil in Dutch oven over medium-high heat. Cook chicken, onion and garlic in oil about 5 minutes, stirring occasionally, until chicken is no longer pink in center.

2. Stir in remaining ingredients except pasta. Heat to boiling. Stir in pasta; reduce heat. Simmer uncovered about 15 minutes or until vegetables and pasta are tender.

1 Serving: Calories 375; Fat 9g; Cholesterol 60mg; Sodium 1580mg; Carbohydrate 39g (Dietary Fiber 3g); Protein 37g

13

Zesty Skillet Chicken
You Can't Live Without!

4 servings

4 skinless, boneless chicken
   breast halves (about 1 pound)

1/4 cup ranch dressing

1/3 cup Italian-style or regular
   dry bread crumbs

2 tablespoons olive or
   vegetable oil

1. Dip chicken into dressing, then coat with bread crumbs.

2. Heat oil in 12-inch nonstick skillet over medium-high heat. Cook chicken in oil 12 to 15 minutes, turning once, until outside is golden brown and juice is no longer pink when centers of thickest pieces are cut.

1 Serving: Calories 290; Fat 16g; Cholesterol 70mg; Sodium 260mg; Carbohydrate 8g (Dietary Fiber 0g); Protein 28g

Skillet Lasagna
You Can't Live Without!

8 servings

1 pound ground beef

1 medium onion, chopped
(1/2 cup)

1 medium green bell pepper,
chopped (1 cup)

3 cups uncooked mafalda
(mini-lasagna noodles)
pasta (6 ounces)

2 1/2 cups water

1/2 teaspoon Italian seasoning

1 jar (30 ounces) spaghetti or
marinara sauce

1 jar (4.5 ounces) sliced
mushrooms, drained

1. Cook beef, onion and bell pepper in 12-inch skillet or
Dutch oven over medium-high heat about 6 minutes,
stirring occasionally, until beef is brown; drain.

2. Stir in remaining ingredients. Heat to boiling, stirring
occasionally; reduce heat to low. Simmer uncovered
10 to 12 minutes or until pasta is tender.

1 Serving: Calories 280; Fat 13g; Cholesterol 30mg; Sodium 810mg;
Carbohydrate 20g (Dietary Fiber 3g); Protein 15g

15

10-Minute Pork Lo Mein
You Can't Live Without!

4 servings

1 tablespoon vegetable oil

*3/4 pound pork tenderloin,
cut into 1/8-inch strips*

*2 packages (3 ounces each)
pork-flavored ramen noodles*

1 1/2 cups water

*1 medium bell pepper, cut into
3/4-inch pieces*

1 cup broccoli flowerets

*4 medium green onions, cut into
1-inch pieces (1/2 cup)*

1 tablespoon soy sauce

1. Heat oil in 12-inch skillet or wok over medium-high heat. Add pork; stir-fry about 5 minutes or until pork is no longer pink.

2. Gently break apart noodles. Stir noodles, seasonings from flavor packets, water, bell pepper, broccoli, onions and soy sauce into pork. Heat to boiling. Boil 3 to 4 minutes, stirring occasionally, until noodles are completely softened.

1 Serving: Calories 335; Fat 13g; Cholesterol 55mg; Sodium 1280mg; Carbohydrate 31g (Dietary Fiber 2g); Protein 25g

16

Home-Style Scrambled Eggs
You Can't Live Without!

4 servings

6 eggs

3/4 teaspoon salt

3 tablespoons water

1/4 cup (1/2 stick) margarine,
   butter or spread

1 cup refrigerated diced potatoes
   with onions or frozen hash
   brown potatoes

1 small zucchini, chopped
   (1 cup)

1 medium tomato, seeded and
   chopped (3/4 cup)

1. Beat eggs, salt and water.

2. Melt margarine in 10-inch skillet over medium heat. Cook potatoes, zucchini and tomato in margarine, stirring occasionally, until hot.

3. Pour egg mixture over vegetable mixture. As mixture begins to set at bottom and side, gently lift cooked portions with spatula so that thin, uncooked portion can flow to bottom. Do not stir. Cook 3 to 5 minutes or until eggs are thickened throughout but still moist.

1 Serving: Calories 250; Fat 19g; Cholesterol 320mg; Sodium 630mg; Carbohydrate 11g (Dietary Fiber 1g); Protein 10g

17

Quick Picante Chili
You Can't Live Without!

4 servings

1 medium onion, chopped
   (1/2 cup)

1 medium green bell pepper,
   chopped (1 cup)

1/8 teaspoon garlic powder

1/2 pound ground beef or pork

1 cup salsa

1 teaspoon chili powder

1 can (15 to 16 ounces) kidney
   or pinto beans, rinsed and
   drained

1 can (16 ounces) whole
   tomatoes, undrained

1. Cook onion, bell pepper, garlic and meat in 3-quart saucepan over medium heat, stirring frequently, until meat is brown; drain if necessary.

2. Stir in remaining ingredients, breaking up tomatoes. Heat to boiling; reduce heat to low. Cover and simmer 10 minutes.

1 Serving: Calories 280; Fat 10g; Cholesterol 35mg; Sodium 850mg; Carbohydrate 37g (Dietary Fiber 10g); Protein 20g

18

Easy Macaroni and Cheese
You Can't Live Without!

4 servings

2 *cups uncooked small shell or elbow macaroni (about 8 ounces)*

1 *cup milk*

1 1/2 *cups shredded Cheddar cheese (6 ounces) or 8-ounce process cheese loaf, cut into cubes*

1/2 *teaspoon salt*

1/2 *teaspoon dry mustard*

1/4 *teaspoon pepper*

1 *tablespoon margarine or butter, if desired*

1. Cook macaroni as directed on package; drain. Stir in remaining ingredients.

2. Cook over low heat, stirring occasionally, about 5 minutes or until cheese is melted and sauce is desired consistency.

1 Serving: Calories 465g; Fat 19g; Cholesterol 50mg; Sodium 620mg; Carbohydrate 54g (Dietary Fiber 2g); Protein 21g

19

3-Step Enchiladas
You Can't Live Without!

5 servings

1 cup sour cream

1 jar (15 to 16 ounces) red or
  green salsa

10 corn or flour tortillas
  (6 to 8 inches in diameter)

2 1/2 cups shredded cooked
  chicken or refried beans

1 cup shredded Monterey Jack
  cheese (4 ounces)

Sour cream

1. Heat oven to 350°. Stir 1 cup sour cream into salsa. Dip each tortilla into sauce to coat both sides.

2. Spoon 1/4 cup of the chicken onto each tortilla; roll up. Place seam sides down in ungreased rectangular baking dish, 13 × 9 × 2 inches. Pour remaining sauce over enchiladas. Sprinkle with cheese.

3. Bake uncovered about 15 minutes or until cheese is melted. Serve with sour cream.

1 Serving: Calories 485; Fat 26g; Cholesterol 135mg; Sodium 810mg; Carbohydrate 31g (Dietary Fiber 4g); Protein 36g

Chicken Pasta Primavera
You Can't Live Without!

4 servings

8 ounces uncooked fettuccine

2 cups broccoli flowerets

1 medium carrot, thinly sliced

1 teaspoon olive or vegetable oil

1 pound boneless, skinless
  chicken breast halves, cut
  into 1/2-inch strips

2/3 cups fat-free ranch dressing

1/4 cup grated Parmesan cheese

1/4 teaspoon garlic powder

1/4 teaspoon dried basil leaves

1. Cook fettuccine as directed on package—except add broccoli and carrot 2 minutes before pasta is done. Drain; return to pan.

2. While pasta is cooking, heat oil in 10-inch nonstick skillet over medium-high heat. Cook chicken in oil 2 to 3 minutes, stirring frequently, until chicken is no longer pink in center.

3. Add chicken and remaining ingredients to fettuccine and vegetables; toss until fettuccine is evenly coated with dressing.

1 Serving: Calories 445; Fat 8g; Cholesterol 110mg; Sodium 600mg; Carbohydrate 60g (Dietary Fiber 3g); Protein 36g

21

Chapter 2

Lighter Fare

 meatless

Fix-It-Faster!

Top a block of cream cheese with salsa,
pepper jelly or chutney and serve with crackers.

Mix salsas, chutneys or preserves into sour cream, plain yogurt
or softened cream cheese and serve as a dip or a spread.

Top tortillas with your choice of shredded cheese, chopped tomatoes,
chopped onion, sour cream, salsa, leftover meats or vegetables.
Microwave or heat in a conventional oven until warm, roll up and enjoy!

Fix a quick mini pizza using tortillas, bagels, English muffins,
crackers, rice cakes or hard rolls as the crust. Top with pizza sauce
and your favorite toppings, then microwave or broil until warm.

Purchase precut fruits and vegetables at the deli or
produce aisle for dipping.

Split leftover biscuits, popovers or croissants and top
with shredded cheese and chopped green chilies.
Broil or bake until cheese is melted.

Freeze flavored yogurt in small paper cups. Add a
stick if you want to make a popsicle. This is a nutritious
afterschool snack or even dessert.

Pesto Tomato Toasts

6 servings

6 slices French bread, 1 inch thick

1/3 cup pesto

1 small tomato, seeded and chopped (1/2 cup)

1/2 cup shredded mozzarella cheese (2 ounces)

1. Heat oven to 375°.

2. Place bread on ungreased cookie sheet. Spread each slice with scant tablespoon of pesto. Top each with tomato; sprinkle with cheese. Bake about 8 minutes or until hot and cheese is melted.

1 Serving: Calories 175; Fat 11g; Cholesterol 5mg; Sodium 250mg; Carbohydrate 14g (Dietary Fiber 1g); Protein 6g

25

Bell Pepper Nachos

6 servings

1/2 green bell pepper, seeded
and cut into 6 strips

1/2 red bell pepper, seeded and
cut into 6 strips

1/2 yellow bell pepper, seeded
and cut into 6 strips

3/4 cup shredded Monterey Jack
cheese (3 ounces)

2 tablespoons chopped ripe
olives

1/4 teaspoon crushed red pepper

1. Line broilerproof pie or round cake pan, about 9 × 1 1/4 inches with aluminum foil. Cut bell pepper strips crosswise in half. Arrange close together in pan. Sprinkle with cheese, olives and red pepper.

2. Set oven control to broil. Broil peppers with tops 3 to 4 inches from heat about 3 minutes or until cheese is melted.

1 Serving: Calories 65; Fat 5g; Cholesterol 15mg; Sodium 110mg; Carbohydrate 2g (Dietary Fiber 0g); Protein 3g

26

Mexican Dip

Makes 3 1/2 cups dip

1/2 pound ground beef

1/2 teaspoon ground mustard
(dry)

1/4 to 1/2 teaspoon chili powder

1 small onion, finely chopped
(1/4 cup)

1/4 cup finely chopped green
bell pepper

1 can (16 ounces) refried beans*

1 can (8 ounces) tomato sauce

1 envelope (1 1/4 ounces) taco
seasoning mix

Sour Cream Topping (right)

Finely shredded lettuce

Shredded Cheddar cheese

Tortilla chips, if desired

1. Cook beef in 10-inch skillet, stirring occasionally, until brown; drain.

2. Stir in mustard, chili powder, onion, bell pepper, beans, tomato sauce and seasoning mix (dry). Heat to boiling, stirring constantly.

3. Spread beef mixture in ungreased pie plate, 9 × 1 1/4 inches. Spread Sour Cream Topping over beef mixture. Sprinkle with lettuce and cheese. Serve with tortilla chips.

*1 can (15 ounces) black beans, rinsed and drained, can be substituted for the refried beans.

SOUR CREAM TOPPING

1 cup sour cream

2 tablespoons shredded Cheddar cheese

1/4 teaspoon chili powder

Mix all ingredients.

1 Tablespoon: Calories 35; Fat 2g; Cholesterol 5mg; Sodium 95mg; Carbohydrate 0g (Dietary Fiber 0g); Protein 1g

28

Garden Vegetable Pizza

8 wedges

*1 container (8 ounces) dill dip
or spinach dip*

*1 package (16 ounces) Italian
bread shell or ready-to-serve
pizza crust (12 to 14 inches
in diameter)*

2 cups chopped raw vegetables*

*1/2 cup shredded Cheddar
cheese (2 ounces)*

Spread dill dip over bread shell to about 1/2 inch from edge. Sprinkle with vegetables and cheese.

*Use vegetables such as bell peppers, broccoli, carrots, cauliflower, tomatoes, green onions and zucchini.

1 Wedge: Calories 235; Fat 9g; Cholesterol 15mg; Sodium 500mg; Carbohydrate 34g (Dietary Fiber 2g); Protein 7g

29

Tex-Mex Pizza

8 wedges

1/4 pound bulk chorizo or spicy pork sausage

1 1/2 cups shredded Monterey Jack cheese (6 ounces)

1 Italian bread shell or purchased pizza crust (12 inches in diameter)

1 jar (8 ounces) salsa (about 1 cup)

1 small bell pepper, chopped (1/2 cup)

1/2 cup canned black beans, rinsed and drained, or 1 can (2 1/4 ounces) sliced ripe olives, drained

1. Heat oven to 450°. Cook sausage in 8-inch skillet over medium-high heat, stirring occasionally, until brown; drain.

2. Sprinkle 1 cup of the cheese over bread shell. Top with salsa, sausage, bell pepper and beans. Sprinkle with remaining cheese.

3. Place on ungreased cookie sheet. Bake 8 to 10 minutes or until pizza is hot and cheese is melted.

1 Wedge: Calories 275; Fat 15g; Cholesterol 35mg; Sodium 680mg; Carbohydrate 26g (Dietary Fiber 3g); Protein 12g

Super Philly Beef Sandwiches

4 sandwiches

2 tablespoons margarine or butter

1 medium onion, coarsely chopped (1/2 cup)

1 1/2 cups sliced mushrooms (4 ounces)*

1/3 cup chopped green bell pepper

4 kaiser rolls, split

1/4 pound thinly sliced, cooked roast beef

4 slices (1 ounce each) provolone cheese

1. Melt margarine in 10-inch skillet over medium-high heat. Cook onion, mushrooms and bell pepper in margarine about 5 minutes, stirring occasionally, until vegetables are tender.

2. Set oven control to broil. Place bottom halves of rolls on ungreased cookie sheet. Top with vegetable mixture, beef and cheese. Broil with tops 4 to 6 inches from heat 2 to 3 minutes or just until cheese is melted. Top with tops of rolls.

*1 can (4 ounces) sliced mushrooms, drained, can be substituted for the fresh mushrooms.

1 Sandwich: Calories 515; Fat 29g; Cholesterol 95mg; Sodium 670mg; Carbohydrate 31g (Dietary Fiber 2g); Protein 35g

32

Honey Ham Bagel Sandwiches

4 open-face sandwiches

2 *pumpernickel bagels, split and toasted*

4 *teaspoons honey mustard*

4 *slices (1 ounce each) fully cooked honey baked ham*

4 *thin slices (1/2 ounce each) Swiss cheese*

Chile pepper rings, if desired

1. Heat oven to 400°. Spread each bagel half with 1 teaspoon mustard. Top each with ham and cheese.

2. Place on cookie sheet. Bake 3 to 5 minutes or until cheese is melted. Top with chile pepper rings.

1 Sandwich: Calories 185; Fat 7g; Cholesterol 30mg; Sodium 620mg; Carbohydrate 18g (Dietary Fiber 1g); Protein 13g

Open-Face Garden Turkey Sandwiches

4 open-face sandwiches

4 cups frozen stir-fry bell peppers and onions (from 16-ounce package)

4 uncooked turkey breast slices, about 1/4 inch thick (1 pound)

1/2 cup shredded Cheddar cheese (2 ounces)

4 tablespoons sandwich spread, mayonnaise or salad dressing

4 slices pumpernickel bread, toasted

1. Spray 12-inch nonstick skillet with nonstick cooking spray; heat over medium-high heat. Cook stir-fry vegetables in skillet 3 to 5 minutes, stirring frequently, until tender. Remove vegetables from skillet.

2. Cook turkey 10 to 12 minutes, turning occasionally, in same skillet until light golden brown and no longer pink in center. Remove from heat.

3. Top each turkey slice with vegetables and cheese. Cover 1 to 2 minutes or until cheese is melted. Spread sandwich spread on bread. Top each slice bread with turkey topped with vegetables and cheese.

1 Open-Face Sandwich: Calories 330; Fat 14g; Cholesterol 95mg; Sodium 490mg; Carbohydrate 21g (Dietary Fiber 3g); Protein 33g

Dressy French Chicken Sandwiches

6 servings

2 cups cubed cooked chicken

1/2 cup chopped red bell pepper
   (about 1 small)

1/2 cup chopped cucumber

1/2 cup shredded mozzarella
   cheese (2 ounces)

1/2 cup mayonnaise or salad
   dressing

2 teaspoons chopped fresh or
   1/2 teaspoon dried oregano
   leaves

1 can (4 1/4 ounces) chopped
   ripe olives, drained

1 baguette (14 to 16 inches),
   cut horizontally in half*

1. Set oven control to broil.

2. Mix all ingredients except baguette. Spoon about
   1 1/2 cups chicken mixture onto each bread half.

3. Place on ungreased cookie sheet. Broil with tops 4 to
   6 inches from heat about 5 minutes or until hot. Cut
   each into 3 slices.

*A baguette is a traditional French bread that's long and thin
and can be up to 2 feet long. Many supermaket bakery sections
carry fresh baguettes. If they are unavailable, you can also use
regular French bread.

1 Serving: Calories 415; Fat 14g; Cholesterol 50mg; Sodium 750mg;
Carbohydrate 48g (Dietary Fiber 2g); Protein 24g

Grilled Vegetable Tortillas

6 servings

1/2 cup diced red bell pepper

1/2 cup diced yellow bell pepper

1/2 cup diced zucchini or chayote

6 flour tortillas (8 or 10 inches in diameter)

1 1/2 cups shredded Monterey Jack cheese (6 ounces)

1 tablespoon margarine or butter

1. Mix bell peppers and zucchini. Spoon about 1/4 cup of the vegetable mixture down center of each tortilla. Top with 1/4 cup of the cheese. Fold tortilla into thirds over filling.

2. Melt margarine in 10-inch skillet over medium heat. Place 3 filled tortillas at a time, seam sides down, in margarine. Cook about 6 minutes, turning after 3 minutes, until golden brown.

1 Serving: Calories 265; Fat 14g; Cholesterol 30mg; Sodium 400mg; Carbohydrate 25g (Dietary Fiber 1g); Protein 11g

37

Speedy Shrimp Quesadillas

8 servings

8 *flour tortillas (8 to 10 inches in diameter)*

2 *cups shredded Monterey Jack cheese with jalapeño peppers (8 ounces)*

1 *large tomato, chopped (1 cup)*

1/2 *cup bacon-flavor bits*

1 *package (4 ounces) frozen cooked salad shrimp, rinsed and thawed*

1. Heat 10-inch nonstick skillet over medium-high heat. Place 1 tortilla in skillet. Sprinkle with 1/4 cup of the cheese and one-fourth each of the tomato, bacon and shrimp. Sprinkle with additional 1/4 cup of the cheese. Top with another tortilla.

2. Cook 1 to 2 minutes or until bottom is golden brown; turn. Cook 1 to 2 minutes longer or until bottom is golden brown.

3. Repeat 3 more times with remaining ingredients. Cut each quesadilla into wedges.

1 Serving: Calories 280; Fat 14g; Cholesterol 50mg; Sodium 490mg; Carbohydrate 25g (Dietary Fiber 1g); Protein 14g

Chapter 3

Pronto Soups and Main-Dish Salads

 meatless

Fix-It-Faster!

Add leftover meats and vegetables to canned or prepared dry soup mixes; then spark their flavor with herbs.

Serve thick cream soups in hollowed-out hard rolls. Use the hollowed-out bread to serve with the soup, as croutons, or as "dunking bread." When you finish your soup, you can also eat the bowl.

Looking for a simple supper chowder? Add leftover cooked vegetables and cooked fish or seafood to a prepared cream-based soup.

Use leftover pasta to make pasta salads and in soups.

For an easy main dish poultry salad, combine chopped cooked poultry and equal parts mayonnaise or plain yogurt and your favorite salad dressing.

Arrange sliced cooked poultry and fresh fruit on a platter for a main-dish salad, or toss cut-up cooked poultry with greens.

Spicy Noodle Soup

6 servings

3 cans (14 1/2 ounces each) ready-to-serve vegetable broth

1 jar (16 ounces) salsa

1 can (15 ounces) black beans, rinsed and drained

1 can (11 ounces) vacuum-packed whole kernel corn, drained

1 package (5 ounces) Japanese curly noodles

1/3 cup chopped fresh cilantro or parsley

1 tablespoon lime juice

1 teaspoon chili powder

1/4 teaspoon ground cumin

1/4 teaspoon pepper

2 tablespoons grated Parmesan cheese

1. Heat broth to boiling in Dutch oven. Stir in remaining ingredients except cheese; reduce heat to medium.

2. Cook 5 to 6 minutes, stirring occasionally, until noodles are tender. Sprinkle with cheese.

1 Serving: Calories 345; Fat 7g; Cholesterol 40mg; Sodium 1240mg; Carbohydrate 58g (Dietary Fiber 10g); Protein 23g

Tex-Mex Minestrone Soup

5 servings

1 package (16 ounces) frozen garlic-seasoned pasta and vegetables

1 jar (16 ounces) thick-and-chunky salsa (2 cups)

1 can (15 ounces) black beans, rinsed and drained

1 can (2 1/4 ounces) sliced ripe olives, drained

2 cups water

1 teaspoon chili powder

1 cup shredded Cheddar cheese (4 ounces)

Sour cream, if desired

1. Mix all ingredients except cheese and sour cream in Dutch oven or 4-quart saucepan. Heat to boiling; reduce heat to low.

2. Simmer uncovered 5 to 7 minutes, stirring occasionally, until vegetables are tender.

3. Top each serving with cheese and sour cream.

1 Serving: Calories 215; Fat 10g; Cholesterol 25mg; Sodium 940mg; Carbohydrate 26g (Dietary Fiber 8g); Protein 13g

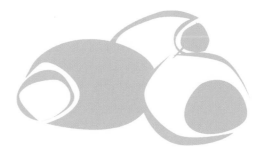

Italian Bean Soup

6 servings

1 teaspoon vegetable oil

1 medium onion, chopped
(about 1/2 cup)

1 clove garlic, crushed

1 1/2 cups chopped fully cooked
smoked reduced-sodium ham
(about 3/4 pound)

1 cup uncooked elbow macaroni
(about 4 ounces)

1/2 teaspoon Italian seasoning

1/8 teaspoon red pepper sauce

3 roma (plum) tomatoes, seeded
and chopped (about 1 cup)

1 medium stalk celery, cut into
1/4-inch diagonal slices
(about 1/2 cup)

2 cans (14 1/2 ounces each)
1/3-less-salt clear chicken
broth

1 can (15 to 16 ounces) great
northern beans, rinsed and
drained

1. Heat oil in 3-quart saucepan over medium-high heat. Cook onion and garlic in oil, stirring frequently, until onion is tender. Stir in remaining ingredients. Heat to boiling; reduce heat.

2. Cover and simmer 12 to 15 minutes or until macaroni is tender.

1 Serving: Calories 225; Fat 4g; Cholesterol 20mg; Sodium 450mg; Carbohydrate 35g (Dietary Fiber 4g); Protein 16g

45

Tortellini Vegetable Chowder

8 servings

1 tablespoon margarine or
  butter

1 large onion, chopped (1 cup)

3 cups water

1 teaspoon dried marjoram
  leaves

1/4 teaspoon coarsely ground
  pepper

1 package (9 ounces) refrigerated
  filled tortellini (any flavor)

2 medium potatoes, peeled and
  cut into 1/2-inch cubes

8 ounces fully cooked smoked
  ham, cut into 1/2-inch pieces
  (about 1 1/3 cups)

1 can (16 1/2 ounces) cream-
  style corn

1 can (11 ounces) whole kernel
  corn with red and green
  peppers, undrained

1 can (12 ounces) evaporated
  milk

1. Melt margarine in 4-quart saucepan over medium heat. Cook onion in margarine, stirring occasionally, until tender. Add water, marjoram and pepper; heat to boiling.

2. Add tortellini and potatoes. Heat to boiling; reduce heat to low. Cover and simmer about 15 minutes, stirring occasionally, until potatoes are tender.

3. Stir in remaining ingredients. Heat to boiling; reduce heat to low. Simmer uncovered 5 minutes.

1 Serving: Calories 290; Fat 11g; Cholesterol 55mg, Sodium 720mg; Carbohydrate 36g (Dietary Fiber 3g); Protein 15g

Creamy Fish Chowder

8 servings

2 medium potatoes, cubed

2 medium carrots, cut into 1/4-inch slices

1 medium onion, chopped

1 cup clam juice

1 cup water

1 tablespoon reduced-calorie margarine

1/2 teaspoon salt

1/4 teaspoon pepper

1 pound haddock or other lean fish fillets, cut into 1-inch pieces

1 can (6 1/2 ounces) whole clams, undrained

1 can (12 ounces) evaporated skim milk

2 tablespoons chopped fresh chives

1 teaspoon paprika

1. Heat potatoes, carrots, onion, clam juice, water, margarine, salt and pepper to boiling in 3-quart saucepan; reduce heat. Cover and simmer 15 to 20 minutes or until potatoes are almost tender.

2. Stir in fish and clams. Cover and heat to boiling; reduce heat. Simmer about 5 minutes or until fish flakes easily with fork.

3. Stir in milk, chives and paprika; heat through.

1 Serving: Calories 225; Fat 2g; Cholesterol 35mg; Sodium 1070mg; Carbohydrate 32g (Dietary Fiber 2g); Protein 19g

47

Ham 'n Corn Chowder

4 servings

1/2 cup chopped thinly sliced
fully cooked ham

1 1/2 cups milk

1 package (16 ounces) frozen
whole kernel corn

1 can (10 3/4 ounces) condensed
cream of celery soup

2 medium green onions, sliced
(1/4 cup)

1. Mix ham, milk, corn and soup in 3-quart saucepan. Heat to boiling, stirring occasionally; reduce heat to low.

2. Simmer uncovered 10 minutes, stirring occasionally. Sprinkle with onions.

1 Serving: Calories 225; Fat 7g; Cholesterol 25mg; Sodium 900mg; Carbohydrate 33g (Dietary Fiber 4g); Protein 11g

48

Speedy Beef Stew

6 servings

1 pound beef cubed steaks

2 teaspoons vegetable oil

3 cups beef broth

1 cup baby-cut carrots

1 cup frozen small whole
onions, thawed

2 teaspoons caraway seed

1/8 teaspoon pepper

1 pound small red potatoes,
cut into fourths

1 jar (12 ounces) baby corn,
drained

3 tablespoons cornstarch

1. Cut beef steaks into 1-inch squares. Heat oil in 3-quart saucepan or Dutch oven over medium-high heat. Cook beef in oil about 5 minutes, stirring frequently, until brown.

2. Stir in 2 1/2 cups of the broth and the remaining ingredients except corn and cornstarch. Heat to boiling; reduce heat. Cover and simmer about 20 minutes or until beef and vegetables are tender. Stir in corn.

3. Mix cornstarch and remaining 1/2 cup broth; stir into stew. Cook about 3 minutes, stirring constantly, until thickened.

1 Serving: Calories 275; Fat 7g; Cholesterol 40mg; Sodium 550mg; Carbohydrate 35g (Dietary Fiber 3g); Protein 21g

50

Quick Garden Chicken Salad

6 servings

1 package (14 ounces) fusilli
   pasta

2 cups cubed cooked chicken

1 cup chopped cucumber
   (about 1 small)

1 cup chopped yellow or red
   bell pepper (about 1 medium)

1 cup chopped tomato (about
   1 large)

3/4 cup spicy eight-vegetable
   juice

1/4 cup lemon juice

1/2 teaspoon freshly ground
   pepper

1/4 teaspoon salt

1 clove garlic, finely chopped

1. Cook pasta as directed on package. Rinse with cold
   water; drain.

2. Mix pasta and remaining ingredients. Serve immediately.

1 Serving: Calories 360; Fat 4g; Cholesterol 40mg; Sodium 510mg;
Carbohydrate 58g (Dietary Fiber 3g); Protein 23g

Chicken and Berries Salad

4 servings

4 cups bite-size pieces mixed
    salad greens (iceberg, Bibb,
    romaine or spinach)

2 cups cut-up cooked chicken

1 cup raspberries*

1/2 cup sliced strawberries*

1/4 cup thinly sliced leek

1/4 cup sliced almonds, toasted

Fruity Yogurt Dressing (right)

Freshly ground pepper

1. Toss salad greens, chicken, berries and leek. Sprinkle with almonds.

2. Serve with Fruity Yogurt Dressing and pepper.

FRUITY YOGURT DRESSING

1 cup plain nonfat yogurt

1/4 cup raspberries*

1/4 cup sliced strawberries*

1 tablespoon raspberry or red wine vinegar

2 teaspoons sugar

Place all ingredients in blender or food processor. Cover and blend on high speed about 15 seconds or process until smooth.

*Frozen unsweetened loose-pack raspberries and strawberries can be substituted for the fresh raspberries and strawberries.

1 Serving: Calories 230; Fat 8g; Cholesterol 60mg; Sodium 110mg; Carbohydrate 17g (Dietary Fiber 5g); Protein 26g

Chicken-Pasta Salad with Pesto

4 servings

6 ounces uncooked multicolored farfalle (bow-tie shape) pasta (about 2 1/4 cups)

1 1/2 cups cut-up cooked chicken

1/4 cup oil-packed sun-dried tomatoes, drained and chopped

1 medium bell pepper, cut into strips

1 small zucchini, thinly sliced

1/2 small red onion, sliced

1/3 cup prepared pesto

1. Cook pasta as directed on package; drain. Rinse with cold water; drain.

2. Mix pasta, chicken, tomatoes, bell pepper, zucchini and onion in large bowl. Stir in pesto.

1 Serving: Calories 580; Fat 15g; Cholesterol 45mg; Sodium 550mg; Carbohydrate 80g (Dietary Fiber 3g); Protein 30g

54

Tuna-Vegetable Salad

6 servings

1 can (12 ounces) tuna, drained

1 package (14 ounces) frozen
   pre-cooked salad tortellini,
   rinsed and drained

1 package (16 ounces) frozen
   broccoli, cauliflower and
   carrots, thawed

1/2 cup creamy Parmesan or
   cucumber dressing

Toss together all ingredients.

1 Serving: Calories 185; Fat 11g; Cholesterol 20mg; Sodium 430mg; Carbohydrate 6g (Dietary Fiber 1g); Protein 16g

Turkey Taco Salad

4 servings

3/4 pound ground turkey breast

1/4 teaspoon garlic powder

2 tablespoons all-purpose flour

1 can (15 ounces) chili beans, undrained

1 tablespoon ground cumin

1 1/2 teaspoons chili powder

1/2 teaspoon onion salt

1/8 teaspoon pepper

6 cups bite-size pieces iceberg lettuce

1 medium onion, chopped

1 medium green bell pepper, chopped

2 medium tomatoes, chopped

1/2 cup shredded reduced-fat Cheddar cheese (4 ounces)

2/3 cup salsa

1/3 cup reduced-calorie Catalina dressing

1 cup nonfat sour cream

1. Cook ground turkey in 10-inch nonstick skillet over medium heat, stirring occasionally, until no longer pink. (If turkey sticks to skillet, add up to 2 tablespoons water.) Stir in garlic, flour, beans, cumin, chili powder, onion salt and pepper. Cook about 5 minutes or until thickened and bubbly.

2. Divide lettuce among 4 plates. Top with turkey mixture, onions, bell pepper, tomatoes and cheese. Mix salsa and dressing; serve with salad. Top salad with sour cream.

1 Serving: Calories 410; Fat 12g; Cholesterol 60mg, Sodium 1100mg; Carbohydrate 46g (Dietary Fiber 9g); Protein 38g

Couscous-Vegetable Salad

6 servings

1 cup uncooked couscous

1 tablespoon olive or vegetable oil

1 medium zucchini, cut into 1/4-inch slices (2 cups)

1 medium yellow summer squash, cut into 1/4-inch slices (1 1/2 cups)

1 large red bell pepper, cut into 1-inch pieces

1/2 medium red onion, cut into 8 wedges

1 container (7 ounces) refrigerated pesto with sun-dried tomatoes or regular pesto

2 tablespoons balsamic or cider vinegar

1. Prepare couscous as directed on package.

2. Meanwhile, heat oil in 10-inch nonstick skillet over medium-high heat. Cook zucchini, yellow squash, bell pepper and onion in oil about 5 minutes, stirring frequently, until crisp-tender.

3. Toss couscous, vegetable mixture, pesto and vinegar in large bowl. Serve warm or cool.

1 Serving: Calories 315; Fat 20g; Cholesterol 5mg; Sodium 105mg; Carbohydrate 30g (Dietary Fiber 3g); Protein 7g

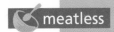

Quick Caesar Salad

6 servings

1/2 cup Caesar dressing

1 large or 2 small bunches
romaine, torn into bite-size
pieces (10 cups)

1 cup Caesar or garlic-flavored
croutons

1/3 cup freshly grated Parmesan
cheese

Freshly ground pepper

Pour dressing into large salad bowl. Add romaine; toss until coated with dressing. Sprinkle with croutons, cheese and pepper; toss.

1 Serving: Calories 165; Fat 13g; Cholesterol 5mg; Sodium 340mg, Carbohydrate 9g (Dietary Fiber 1g); Protein 4g

59

Greek Salad

6 servings

Vinegar Dressing (right)

1 medium head lettuce, torn into bite-size pieces

1 bunch romaine, torn into bite-size pieces

1 bunch green onions, cut into 1/2-inch pieces

1 medium cucumber, sliced

24 pitted Greek or ripe olives

10 radishes, sliced

1 cup crumbled feta or chèvre (goat) cheese (4 ounces)

1 medium carrot, shredded (3/4 cup)

Prepare Vinegar Dressing. Toss dressing and remaining ingredients except cheese and carrot. Sprinkle salad with cheese and carrot.

VINEGAR DRESSING

1/2 cup olive or vegetable oil

1/3 cup wine vinegar

1 tablespoon chopped fresh or 1 teaspoon dried oregano leaves

1/2 teaspoon salt

Shake all ingredients in tightly covered container.

1 Serving: Calories 280; Fat 26g; Cholesterol 20mg; Sodium 880mg; Carbohydrate 9g (Dietary Fiber 4g); Protein 6g

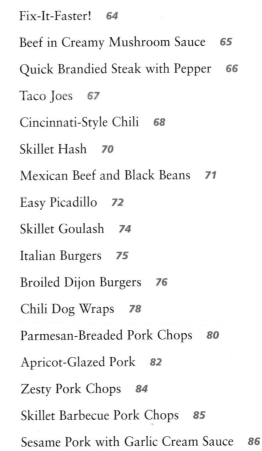

Chapter 4

Quick Meaty Main Dishes

 meatless

Fix-It-Faster!

Microwave ground beef or pork in a microwavable dish to use for main dish recipes. Crumble 1 pound into dish; cover loosely and microwave on high 5 to 6 minutes, stirring after 3 minutes, until no longer pink. Drain fat and continue with the recipe.

Keep frozen cooked meatballs and prepared spaghetti sauce on hand to heat quickly and serve over your favorite pasta.

Heat equal amounts Cheddar cheese soup and beer to use as a sauce for cooked meatballs or cubed cooked ham. Serve over rice or pasta.

Prepare a quick beef stroganoff by heating leftover beef mixed with equal amounts of cream of mushroom soup and sour cream.

Wrap cooked smoked sausage in (thawed) frozen puff pastry and bake according to the pastry direction for an impressive main dish or appetizer.

Grill extra steaks, chops or burgers to reheat later in the microwave (or freeze and reheat).

Heat sliced or cubed meat with leftover gravy and serve over biscuits, corn bread, popovers or baked potatoes.

Beef in Creamy Mushroom Sauce

6 servings

2 tablespoons cornstarch

1 cup water

1 pound lean beef boneless
sirloin steak, about 1/2 inch
thick

1 small onion, chopped

1 clove garlic, crushed

1/4 teaspoon salt

1/8 teaspoon pepper

1 medium red bell pepper,
chopped

3 cups sliced mushrooms
(about 8 ounces)

1/4 cup brandy or water

1 teaspoon low-sodium beef
bouillon granules

2 tablespoons nonfat sour
cream

3 tablespoons chopped fresh
chives

3 cups hot cooked mostaccioli

1. Stir cornstarch into water; reserve. Trim fat from beef steak. Cut beef into thin strips, about 1 1/2 × 1/2 inch. Spray 10-inch skillet with nonstick cooking spray; heat over medium-high heat. Cook onion, garlic, salt and pepper in skillet about 3 minutes, stirring frequently, until onion is tender.

2. Stir in beef and bell pepper. Cook about 4 minutes, stirring frequently, until beef is no longer pink. Stir in mushrooms. Add brandy to skillet; sprinkle bouillon granules over beef mixture. Heat to boiling; reduce heat. Cover and simmer 1 minute.

3. Stir in sour cream. Stir in cornstarch mixture. Cook over medium-high heat about 2 minutes, stirring frequently, until thickened. Stir in chives. Serve over mostaccioli.

1 Serving: Calories 205; Fat 3g; Cholesterol 40mg; Sodium 220mg; Carbohydrate 27g (Dietary Fiber 2g); Protein 19g

65

Quick Brandied Steak with Pepper

4 servings

1 teaspoon cracked black
    pepper

3/4 teaspoon chopped fresh or
    1/4 teaspoon dried basil
    leaves

3/4 teaspoon chopped fresh or
    1/4 teaspoon dried rosemary
    leaves

1/8 teaspoon onion powder

4 beef cubed steaks (5 ounces
    each)

1 tablespoon margarine or
    butter

2 tablespoon brandy or beef
    broth

1/4 cup beef broth

1. Mix pepper, basil, rosemary and onion powder. Rub pepper mixture into both sides of each steak.

2. Melt margarine in 12-inch skillet over medium heat. Cook beef in margarine 7 to 8 minutes, turning occasionally, until medium-rare to medium. Remove beef from skillet; keep warm.

3. Add brandy and broth to skillet. Heat to boiling, stirring to loosen brown bits from bottom of skillet; reduce heat to low. Simmer uncovered 3 to 4 minutes or until slightly thickened. Pour brandy mixture over beef.

1 Serving: Calories 245; Fat 13g; Cholesterol 80mg; Sodium 150mg; Carbohydrate 1g (Dietary Fiber 0g); Protein 31g

Taco Joes

10 servings

1 pound ground beef

1 medium stalk celery, chopped
   (1/2 cup)

1 medium onion, chopped
   (1/2 cup)

1 jar (16 ounces) salsa (2 cups)

1 can (about 15 ounces) whole
   kernel corn, drained

10 taco shells

Shredded lettuce, if desired

1. Cook beef in 10-inch skillet over medium heat 8 to 10 minutes, stirring occasionally, until brown; drain. Stir in celery, onion, salsa and corn. Heat to boiling, stirring constantly; reduce heat. Simmer uncovered 5 minutes, stirring occasionally.

2. Heat taco shells as directed on package. Spoon beef mixture into taco shells. Top with lettuce.

1 Serving: Calories 185; Fat 10g; Cholesterol 25mg; Sodium 290mg; Carbohydrate 17g (Dietary Fiber 3g); Protein 10g

Cincinnati-Style Chili

5 servings

1/2 pound ground beef

1 large onion, chopped (1 cup)

1 can (16 ounces) whole tomatoes, undrained

1 can (15 to 16 ounces) kidney beans, undrained

1 can (8 ounces) tomato sauce

1 tablespoon chili powder

1 package (7 ounces) spaghetti

1 1/4 cups shredded Cheddar cheese (5 ounces)

1. Cook beef and about 3/4 cup of the onions in 3-quart saucepan over medium heat 8 to 10 minutes, stirring occasionally, until beef is brown and onions are tender; drain.

2. Stir in tomatoes, beans, tomato sauce and chili powder; breaking up tomatoes. Cook uncovered over medium heat about 10 minutes, stirring occasionally, until desired consistency.

3. Meanwhile, cook and drain spaghetti as directed on package.

4. For each serving, spoon about 3/4 cup beef mixture over 1 cup hot spaghetti. Sprinkle each serving with 1/4 cup cheese and about 1 tablespoon remaining onion.

1 Serving: Calories 465; Fat 18g; Cholesterol 55mg; Sodium 930mg; Carbohydrate 56g (Dietary Fiber 8g); Protein 28g

Skillet Hash

4 servings

2 cups chopped cooked lean
   beef or corned beef

2 cups frozen country-style hash
   brown potatoes

1 medium onion, chopped
   (1/2 cup)

1 tablespoon chopped fresh
   parsley

1/2 teaspoon salt

1/8 teaspoon pepper

2 to 3 tablespoons vegetable oil

1. Mix beef, potatoes, onion, parsley, salt and pepper.

2. Heat oil in 10-inch skillet over medium heat. Spread beef mixture evenly in skillet. Cook 10 to 15 minutes, turning frequently, until brown.

1 Serving: Calories 325; Fat 19g; Cholesterol 50mg; Sodium 610mg; Carbohydrate 23g (Dietary Fiber 2g); Protein 18g

Mexican Beef and Black Beans

4 servings

1 pound ground beef

1 tablespoon chopped fresh
   parsley or 1 teaspoon dried
   parsley flakes

1 tablespoon white wine vinegar

1 teaspoon grated lime or lemon
   peel

1/4 teaspoon red pepper sauce

1 medium red or green bell
   pepper, chopped (1 cup)

2 medium green onions, thinly
   sliced (1/4 cup)

2 cans (15 ounces each) black
   beans, rinsed and drained

1. Cook beef in 10-inch skillet over medium heat 8 to 10 minutes, stirring occasionally, until brown; drain.

2. Stir in remaining ingredients. Cook about 5 minutes, stirring frequently, until hot.

1 Serving: Calories 465; Fat 17g; Cholesterol 65mg; Sodium 530mg; Carbohydrate 54g (Dietary Fiber 14g); Protein 38g

Easy Picadillo

4 servings

1 pound lean ground beef

1 small green bell pepper,
chopped (1/2 cup)

1 can (14 1/2 ounces) salsa-style
chunky tomatoes, undrained

1 can canned black beans,
rinsed and drained

1/2 cup golden raisins

1. Cook beef and bell pepper in 12-inch nonstick skillet over medium heat 8 to 10 minutes, stirring occasionally, until beef is brown; drain.

2. Stir in remaining ingredients; reduce heat to low. Cover and simmer 5 to 7 minutes, stirring occasionally, until hot.

1 Serving: Calories: 365; Fat 17g; Cholesterol 65mg; Sodium 330mg; Carbohydrate 32g (Dietary Fiber 5g); Protein 26g

72

Skillet Goulash

4 servings

1 pound ground beef

1 1/2 cups uncooked fine egg
noodles (3 ounces)

1/2 cup water

1 medium onion, chopped
(1/2 cup)

1 medium stalk celery, chopped
(1/2 cup)

1 can (15 ounces) Italian-style
tomato sauce

1. Cook beef in 10-inch skillet over medium heat 8 to 10 minutes, stirring occasionally, until brown; drain.

2. Stir in remaining ingredients. Heat to boiling; reduce heat to low. Cover and simmer 15 to 20 minutes, stirring occasionally, until noodles are tender. (Add a small amount of water if necessary.)

1 Serving: Calories 375; Fat 21g; Cholesterol 85mg; Sodium 440mg; Carbohydrate 24g (Dietary Fiber 3g); Protein 25g

Italian Burgers

4 servings

1 pound ground beef or turkey

1/3 cup spaghetti sauce

3 tablespoons finely chopped onion

4 slices (1 ounce each) provolone cheese

8 slices Italian bread

1. Mix meat, spaghetti sauce and onion. Shape mixture into 4 patties, each about 3/4 inch thick.

2. Set oven control to broil. Place patties on rack in broiler pan. Broil with tops about 3 inches from heat 12 minutes, turning once.

3. Top each patty with cheese slice. Broil about 1 minute longer or until beef is no longer pink in center and juice is clear. Serve between bread slices. Serve with additional spaghetti sauce, if desired.

1 Serving: Calories 450; Fat 26g; Cholesterol 90mg; Sodium 690mg; Carbohydrate 23g (Dietary Fiber 1g); Protein 32g

75

Broiled Dijon Burgers

6 sandwiches

2 slices bread, torn into 1-inch
pieces

1/4 cup fat-free egg product or
2 egg whites

2 tablespoons skim milk

3/4 pound extra-lean ground
beef

1/4 teaspoon salt

1/8 teaspoon pepper

1/4 cup finely chopped onion
(about 1 small)

2 teaspoons Dijon mustard

6 sourdough or plain English
muffins, split and lightly
toasted

6 leaves lettuce

6 slices tomato

Dijon-Yogurt Sauce (right)

1. Set oven control to broil. Spray broiler pan rack with
nonstick cooking spray. Mix bread, egg product and
milk in medium bowl. Stir in ground beef, salt, pepper,
onion and mustard. Shape by about 1/3 cupfuls into
6 patties, about 3 1/2 × 1/2 inch. Place on rack in
broiler pan.

2. Broil with tops 3 to 4 inches from heat about 5 minutes or until brown. Turn patties. Broil 3 to 4 minutes
longer or until no longer pink in center.

3. Serve on English muffins with lettuce, tomato and
Dijon-Yogurt Sauce.

DIJON-YOGURT SAUCE

1/2 cup plain nonfat yogurt

1 teaspoon sweet pickle relish

1/2 teaspoon Dijon mustard

Mix all ingredients.

1 Sandwich: Calories 300; Fat 10g; Cholesterol 35mg; Sodium 530mg;
Carbohydrate 35g (Dietary Fiber 2g); Protein 19g

Chili Dog Wraps

5 servings

10 *corn or flour tortillas
(6 to 8 inches in diameter)*

10 *hot dogs*

1 *can (15 to 16 ounces) chili*

2 *cups salsa*

1 *cup shredded Cheddar or
Monterey Jack cheese
(4 ounces)*

1. Heat oven to 350°. Grease rectangular baking dish, 13 × 9 × 2 inches.

2. Soften tortillas as directed on package. Place 1 hot dog and 3 tablespoons chili on each tortilla. Roll up tortillas; place seam side down in baking dish. Spoon salsa over tortillas.

3. Cover and bake 20 minutes. Sprinkle with cheese. Bake uncovered about 5 minutes longer or until cheese is melted.

1 Serving: Calories 550; Fat 36g; Cholesterol 65mg; Sodium 2190mg; Carbohydrate 41g (Dietary Fiber 7g); Protein 22g

Parmesan-Breaded Pork Chops

4 servings

1/3 cup Italian-style dry bread
crumbs

2 tablespoons grated Parmesan
cheese

4 pork boneless butterfly loin
chops, 1/2 inch thick (about
1 1/4 pounds)

1 egg, beaten

1 can (14 1/2 ounces) chunky
tomatoes with olive oil, garlic
and spices, undrained

1 can (8 ounces) tomato sauce

1 small green bell pepper,
chopped (1/2 cup)

1. Mix bread crumbs and cheese. Dip pork in egg, then
   coat with crumb mixture.

2. Spray 12-inch nonstick skillet with nonstick cooking
   spray; heat over medium heat. Cook pork in skillet
   about 5 minutes, turning once, until brown.

3. Stir in remaining ingredients. Heat to boiling, reduce
   heat to low. Cover and simmer 10 to 12 minutes, stirring occasionally, until pork is slightly pink in center.

1 Serving: Calories 245; Fat 10g; Cholesterol 110mg; Sodium 680mg;
Carbohydrate 16g (Dietary Fiber 2g); Protein 25g

Apricot-Glazed Pork

4 servings

1 tablespoon chili oil or
   vegetable oil

1 pound pork tenderloin,
   cut into 1/2-inch slices

1 package (16 ounces) frozen
   broccoli, cauliflower and
   carrots

3 tablespoons apricot preserves

1 tablespoon oyster sauce or
   hoisin sauce

Hot cooked rice or noodles,
   if desired

1. Heat wok or 12-inch skillet over high heat. Add oil;
   rotate wok to coat side.

2. Add pork; stir-fry 4 to 5 minutes or until no longer
   pink. Add broccoli mixture; stir-fry 2 minutes. Stir in
   preserves and oyster sauce; cook and stir about 30 seconds or until hot. Serve with rice.

1 Serving: Calories 235; Fat 8g; Cholesterol 65mg; Sodium 270mg;
Carbohydrate 18g (Dietary Fiber 3g); Protein 26g

Zesty Pork Chops

6 servings

2/3 cup packed brown sugar

1/4 cup prepared horseradish

1 tablespoon lemon juice

6 fully cooked smoked pork chops, about 1/2 inch thick (about 1 1/4 pounds)

1. Set oven control to broil.

2. Heat brown sugar, horseradish and lemon juice to boiling in 1-quart saucepan, stirring constantly. Brush on pork.

3. Place pork on rack in broiler pan. Broil with tops 4 to 6 inches from heat 3 minutes; turn. Broil 3 to 5 minutes longer or until hot.

1 Serving: Calories 265; Fat 8g; Cholesterol 65mg; Sodium 60mg; Carbohydrate 25g (Dietary Fiber 0g); Protein 23g

84

Skillet Barbecue Pork Chops

4 servings

4 *pork loin or rib chops,*
  1/2 inch thick (about
  1 1/4 pounds)

1/4 *teaspoon salt*

1/8 *teaspoon pepper*

1 *can (15 ounces) chunky*
  tomato sauce with onions,
  celery and green bell peppers

2 *tablespoons packed brown*
  sugar

2 *tablespoons vinegar*

2 *tablespoons Worcestershire*
  sauce

1 *teaspoon ground mustard*
  (dry)

1. Spray 12-inch nonstick skillet with nonstick cooking spray; heat over medium heat. Sprinkle both sides of pork with salt and pepper. Cook pork in skillet about 5 minutes, turning once, until brown.

2. Mix remaining ingredients; add to skillet. Heat to boiling; reduce heat to low. Cover and simmer 10 to 15 minutes; stirring occasionally, until pork is slightly pink in center.

1 Serving: Calories 230; Fat 8g; Cholesterol 65mg; Sodium 900mg; Carbohydrate 16g (Dietary Fiber 1g); Protein 24g

85

Sesame Pork with Garlic Cream Sauce

6 servings

1 1/2 pounds pork tenderloin

2 tablespoons vegetable oil

1/4 cup sesame seed

1 tablespoon margarine or butter

2 cloves garlic, finely chopped

1 package (3 ounces) cream cheese, cut into cubes

1/3 cup milk

1 tablespoon chopped fresh or 1 teaspoon freeze-dried chives

1. Cut pork crosswise into 12 slices. Flatten slices to 1/2-inch thickness.

2. Set oven control to broil. Brush pork with oil. Place pork on rack in broiler pan. Sprinkle with half of the sesame seed. Broil pork with tops 4 to 6 inches from heat 6 minutes; turn. Sprinkle with remaining sesame seed. Broil about 5 minutes longer or until pork is no longer pink.

3. Melt margarine in 10-inch skillet over medium heat. Cook garlic in margarine about 2 minutes, stirring occasionally; reduce heat. Add cream cheese and milk. Cook, stirring constantly, until smooth and hot. Stir in chives. Serve sauce with pork.

1 Serving: Calories 285; Fat 19g; Cholesterol 85mg; Sodium 120mg; Carbohydrate 2g (Dietary Fiber 0g); Protein 27g

German Sausage and Sauerkraut

6 servings

1 tablespoon margarine or
   butter

1 pound fully cooked bratwurst

2 cans (16 ounces each)
   sauerkraut, drained

1/4 teaspoon caraway seed,
   if desired

1/3 cup packed brown sugar

1. Melt margarine in 10-inch skillet over medium heat. Cook bratwurst in margarine about 5 minutes, turning frequently, until brown.

2. Add sauerkraut. Sprinkle with caraway seed and brown sugar. Cover and cook over low heat about 10 minutes or until hot.

1 Serving: Calories 330; Fat 24g; Cholesterol 55mg; Sodium 1560mg; Carbohydrate 19g (Dietary Fiber 3g); Protein 12g

Chapter 5

No-Fuss Poultry, Fish and Seafood

meatless

Fix-It-Faster!

Cut up boneless chicken breasts or thighs
and combine with cut-up vegetables from the
produce section, salad bar or deli for a quick stir-fry.

Save time when sautéing poultry, use boneless
chicken breasts or thighs or turkey slices.

Prepare frozen chicken or turkey patties
as directed on the package. Top with spaghetti sauce
and mozzarella cheese. Bake or broil until cheese is melted.

Bake frozen chicken nuggets and add to
casseroles, or serve with your favorite dipping sauce,
such as barbecue or sweet-and-sour.

Serve broiled fish with simple citrus butters
(orange, lemon, lime, grapefruit) instead of complicated
sauces: Mix 1/4 cup margarine or butter, melted,
1 teaspoon grated peel and 2 tablespoons of juice.

For a quick dinner with an Italian flavor, bake frozen
fish sticks or fillets as directed on the package.
Top with pizza sauce and shredded mozzarella cheese.
Bake 2 minutes more or until the cheese melts.

Purchase fish nuggets or fish sticks, and prepare
according to the package directions. Serve with your favorite
dipping sauces—tartar, sweet-and-sour and barbecue.

Spicy Mexican Skillet Chicken

4 servings

1/2 to 1 teaspoon chili powder

1/4 teaspoon salt

1/4 teaspoon pepper

4 boneless, skinless chicken breast halves (about 1 pound)

1 tablespoon vegetable oil

1 cup frozen (thawed) corn or canned (drained) whole kernel corn

1/3 cup chunky salsa

2 tablespoons chopped fresh cilantro

1 large tomato, chopped (about 1 cup)

1 can (15 ounces) black beans, rinsed and drained

1. Mix chili powder, salt and pepper. Sprinkle evenly over both sides of chicken.

2. Heat oil in 10-inch skillet over medium heat until hot. Cook chicken in oil 10 minutes until brown on both sides. Stir in remaining ingredients. Heat to boiling; reduce heat.

3. Cover and simmer 3 to 5 minutes or until juice of chicken is no longer pink when centers of the thickest pieces are cut and vegetables are heated through.

1 Serving: Calories 335; Fat 7g; Cholesterol 60mg; Sodium 800mg; Carbohydrate 42g (Dietary Fiber 9g); Protein 1g

Chicken and Mushrooms
with Spaghetti

4 servings

*4 boneless, skinless chicken
    breast halves (about 1 pound)*

*2 tablespoons olive or vegetable
    oil*

2 cloves garlic, finely chopped

*2 tablespoons finely chopped
    onion*

1 cup sliced fresh mushrooms

*1 medium green bell pepper,
    chopped (about 1 cup)*

*1/2 cup dry white wine or
    chicken broth*

*1 teaspoon red or white wine
    vinegar*

1 jar (14 ounces) spaghetti sauce

Hot cooked pasta, if desired

1. Flatten each chicken breast half to 1/4-inch thickness between sheets of plastic wrap or waxed paper.

2. Heat oil in 10-inch skillet over medium-high heat. Cook garlic, onion, mushrooms and bell pepper in oil 5 minutes, stirring occasionally.

3. Add chicken to skillet. Cook about 8 minutes, turning once, until brown. Add wine and vinegar. Cook 3 minutes. Stir in spaghetti sauce.

4. Cook 10 to 12 minutes or until juice of chicken is no longer pink when centers of thickest pieces are cut. Serve with pasta.

1 Serving: Calories 290; Fat 14g; Cholesterol 60mg; Sodium 810mg; Carbohydrate 14g (Dietary Fiber 1g); Protein 26g

Easy Chicken Paprika

6 servings

1 tablespoon vegetable oil

6 boneless, skinless chicken
    breast halves (about
    1 1/2 pounds)

1 large onion, sliced

1 1/2 cups milk

2 tablespoons paprika

1 can (10 3/4 ounces) condensed
    cream of chicken soup

1 medium bell pepper, cut into
    strips

4 cups hot cooked egg noodles

1. Heat oil in 10-inch skillet over medium heat until hot.
   Cook chicken and onion in oil turning chicken once
   and stirring onion occasionally, until chicken is brown
   and onion is tender; drain.

2. Mix milk, paprika and soup; pour over chicken and
   onion. Stir in bell pepper. Heat to boiling, stirring
   occasionally; reduce heat.

3. Cover and simmer about 15 minutes or until juice of
   chicken is no longer pink when centers of thickest
   pieces are cut. Serve over noodles.

1 Serving: Calories 380; Fat 11g; Cholesterol 185mg; Sodium 660mg;
Carbohydrate 37g (Dietary Fiber 1g); Protein 33g

94

Quick Chicken with Olives and Tomatoes

6 servings

2 tablespoons margarine or butter

2 cloves garlic, crushed

1 small onion, chopped (about 1/4 cup)

6 boneless, skinless chicken breast halves (about 1 1/2 pounds)

1/2 cup red wine vinegar

2 teaspoons chopped fresh or 1/2 teaspoon dried thyme leaves

1/2 teaspoon salt

1/4 teaspoon pepper

2 large tomatoes, chopped (about 2 cups)

1 can (2 1/4 ounces) sliced ripe olives, drained

1. Heat margarine in 10-inch skillet over medium-high heat until melted. Cook garlic, onion and chicken in margarine until chicken is brown on both sides.

2. Stir in remaining ingredients; reduce heat. Cook 10 to 15 minutes or until juice of chicken is no longer pink when centers of thickest pieces are cut.

1 Serving: Calories 200; Fat 8g; Cholesterol 65mg; Sodium 370mg; Carbohydrate 6g (Dietary Fiber 1g); Protein 27g

95

Lemon-Dill Chicken

6 servings

1/4 cup (1/2 stick) margarine or butter

6 skinless, boneless chicken breast halves (about 1 1/2 pounds)

1/2 cup dry white wine or chicken broth

1 tablespoon chopped fresh or 1/2 teaspoon dried dill weed

1 tablespoon lemon juice

1/4 teaspoon salt

1 medium green onion, sliced

1. Melt margarine in 10-inch skillet over medium-high heat. Cook chicken in margarine about 6 minutes, turning once, until light brown.

2. Mix wine, dill weed, lemon juice and salt; pour over chicken. Heat to boiling; reduce heat to low. Cover and simmer 10 to 15 minutes or until juice of chicken is no longer pink when centers of thickest pieces are cut. Remove chicken from skillet; keep warm.

3. Meanwhile, heat wine mixture to boiling. Boil about 3 minutes or until reduced to about half; pour over chicken. Sprinkle with onion.

1 Serving: Calories 200; Fat 11g; Cholesterol 60mg; Sodium 240mg; Carbohydrate 1g (Dietary Fiber 0g); Protein 24g

Everyday Chicken Risotto

6 servings

2 tablespoons olive or vegetable oil

1/3 cup chopped green onions

1 medium carrot, thinly sliced (about 1/2 cup)

2 cloves garlic, finely chopped

1 cup uncooked arborio or regular long grain rice

3 1/2 cups chicken broth

1 tablespoon chopped fresh parsley

1/8 teaspoon saffron threads, crushed, or ground turmeric

2 cups cut-up cooked chicken

1. Heat oil in 3-quart saucepan over medium-high heat. Cook onions, carrot and garlic in oil about 4 to 5 minutes, stirring frequently, until carrots are crisp-tender. Stir in rice. Cook, stirring frequently, until rice begins to brown.

2. Pour 1/2 cup broth, parsley and saffron over rice. Cook uncovered, stirring occasionally, until liquid is absorbed. Continue cooking 15 to 20 minutes, adding broth 1/2 cup at a time and stirring occasionally, until rice is tender and creamy. Stir in chicken; heat through.

1 Serving: Calories 270; Fat 9g; Cholesterol 40mg; Sodium 280mg; Carbohydrate 29g (Dietary Fiber 2g); Protein 19g

Crispy Basil Chicken

6 servings

1/3 cup cholesterol-free egg product

2 tablespoons chicken broth

1 tablespoon Dijon mustard

1 clove garlic, finely chopped

1 1/2 cups dried bread crumbs

1 tablespoon dried basil leaves

1 teaspoon paprika

1/4 teaspoon white pepper

12 boneless, skinless chicken thighs (about 1 1/2 pounds)

1. Heat oven to 400°. Spray shallow roasting pan with nonstick cooking spray.

2. Mix egg product, broth, mustard and garlic in small bowl. Mix bread crumbs, basil, paprika and white pepper in large plastic bag.

3. Dip chicken into egg mixture, then shake in bag to coat with crumb mixture. Place in pan.

4. Bake uncovered about 20 minutes or until juice is no longer pink when centers of thickest pieces are cut.

1 Serving: Calories 305; Fat 10g; Cholesterol 95mg; Sodium 350mg; Carbohydrate 20g (Dietary Fiber 0g); Protein 34g

100

Quick Jambalaya

4 servings

2 teaspoons vegetable oil

1/2 pound skinless, boneless chicken thighs, cut into 3/4-inch cubes

1/2 pound fully cooked reduced-fat turkey kielbasa sausage, cut into 1/4-inch slices

1 medium onion, sliced

1 medium green bell pepper, coarsely chopped

1 medium stalk celery, sliced

1 cup water

1 tablespoon all-purpose flour

1 can (14 1/2 ounces) no-salt-added whole tomatoes, undrained

2 tablespoons steak sauce

1/4 to 1/2 teaspoon red pepper sauce

2 cups cooked brown or white rice

1. Heat oil in nonstick Dutch oven over medium heat. Cook chicken in oil 8 to 10 minutes, stirring occasionally, until light brown. Stir in sausage, onion, bell pepper and celery. Cook, stirring frequently, until vegetables are crisp-tender.

2. Mix water and flour; stir into chicken mixture. Cook, stirring frequently, until slightly thickened.

3. Stir in tomatoes, steak sauce and pepper sauce, breaking up tomatoes. Heat to boiling; reduce heat. Simmer uncovered 10 to 15 minutes. Stir in rice; heat through.

1 Serving: Calories 330; Fat 11g; Cholesterol 80mg; Sodium 1000mg; Carbohydrate 34g (Dietary Fiber 4g); Protein 28g

101

Chinese Chicken Stir-Fry

4 servings

1 tablespoon vegetable oil

1 pound cut-up chicken breast
  for stir-fry

1/2 cup teriyaki baste and glaze

3 tablespoons lemon juice

1 package (16 ounces) frozen
  broccoli, carrots, water
  chestnuts and red peppers

Hot cooked rice, couscous or
  noodles, if desired

1. Heat wok or 12-inch skillet over high heat. Add oil;
   rotate wok to coat side. Add chicken; stir-fry 3 to
   4 minutes or until chicken is no longer pink in center.

2. Stir in remaining ingredients except rice. Heat to boiling, stirring constantly; reduce heat to low. Cover and
   simmer about 6 minutes or until vegetables are crisp-
   tender. Serve with rice.

1 Serving: Calories 245; Fat 7g; Cholesterol 60mg; Sodium 1480mg;
Carbohydrate 21g (Dietary Fiber 3g); Protein 28g

102

Everyday Cassoulet

4 servings

1/2 pound skinless, boneless
   chicken breast halves, cut
   into 1/2-inch pieces

1/2 pound fully cooked Polish
   sausage, cut into 1/2-inch
   slices

1 can (15 to 16 ounces) great
   northern beans, rinsed and
   drained

1 can (15 to 16 ounces) dark
   red kidney beans, rinsed and
   drained

1 can (14 1/2 ounces) chunky
   tomatoes with olive oil, garlic
   and spices, undrained

1 tablespoon packed brown
   sugar

4 medium green onions, sliced

1. Spray 12-inch nonstick skillet with nonstick cooking spray; heat over medium-high heat. Cook chicken 3 to 5 minutes, stirring occasionally, until brown.

2. Stir in remaining ingredients except onions. Cook uncovered over medium-low heat 8 to 10 minutes, stirring occasionally, until chicken is no longer pink in center.

3. Stir in onions. Cook 3 to 5 minutes, stirring occasionally, until onions are crisp-tender.

1 Serving: Calories 485; Fat 19g; Cholesterol 70mg; Sodium 1370mg; Carbohydrate 54g (Dietary Fiber 12g); Protein 37g

Grilled Lime Chicken Breasts

4 servings

1/4 cup frozen (thawed) limeade concentrate

1/4 cup vegetable oil

1 teaspoon finely shredded lime peel, if desired

1/4 teaspoon paprika

4 boneless chicken breast halves (about 1 pound)

1. Heat coals or gas grill. Mix all ingredients except chicken.

2. Place chicken, skin sides up, on grill 4 to 6 inches from medium heat. Brush with limeade mixture.

3. Cover and grill 20 to 25 minutes, brushing frequently with limeade mixture and turning occasionally, until juice of chicken is no longer pink when centers of thickest pieces are cut. Discard any remaining limeade mixture.

1 Serving: Calories 285; Fat 21g; Cholesterol 60mg; Sodium 55mg; Carbohydrate 2g; Protein 22g

Easy Turkey Cacciatore

4 servings

4 uncooked turkey breast slices,
    1/4 inch thick (1 pound)

1/4 cup all-purpose flour

1/4 teaspoon pepper

2 tablespoons olive or vegetable
    oil

1 small onion, sliced

1 small green bell pepper,
    cut into 1/4-inch strips

1 jar (26 ounces) spaghetti sauce

1 package (8 ounces) refrigerated
    fettuccine

1/2 cup shredded mozzarella
    cheese (2 ounces)

1. Coat turkey with flour; sprinkle with pepper.

2. Heat oil in 12-inch skillet over medium-high heat. Cook turkey, onion and bell pepper in oil 10 to 12 minutes, turning once, until turkey is no longer pink in center. Stir in spaghetti sauce. Cook about 5 minutes or until sauce is hot.

3. Cook and drain fettuccine as directed on package. Place fettuccine on 4 serving plates. Top with turkey mixture. Sprinkle with cheese.

1 Serving: Calories 595; Fat 22g; Cholesterol 125mg; Sodium 1400mg; Carbohydrate 63g (Dietary Fiber 5g); Protein 41g

Speedy Turkey Scallopini

4 servings

4 uncooked turkey breast slices,
   1/4 inch thick (1 pound)

1/2 cup all-purpose flour

2 tablespoons vegetable oil

3 tablespoons margarine or
   butter

2 tablespoons lemon juice

Hot cooked spaghetti, if desired

Chopped fresh parsley

Lemon slices, if desired

1. Coat turkey with flour.

2. Heat oil and 2 tablespoons of the margarine in 12-inch skillet over medium heat. Cook turkey in oil mixture about 4 minutes on each side or no longer pink in center. Remove turkey from skillet; keep warm.

3. Melt remaining 1 tablespoon margarine in same skillet. Stir in lemon juice; pour over turkey. Serve over spaghetti. Sprinkle with parsley. Garnish with lemon slices.

1 Serving: Calories 335; Fat 19g; Cholesterol 65mg; Sodium 160mg; Carbohydrate 13g (Dietary Fiber 0g); Protein 28g

Turkey Patties and Vegetables

4 servings

1 orange

1/3 cup Hawaiian or regular
stir-fry sauce

1 tablespoon packed brown
sugar

1 package (1 pound) seasoned
turkey patties

1 package (16 ounces) fresh
stir-fry vegetables

1. Grate 1 teaspoon peel from orange. Peel orange; discard peel. Cut orange into thin wedges or slices. Mix stir-fry sauce, brown sugar and orange peel.

2. Spray 12-inch nonstick skillet with nonstick cooking spray; heat over medium-high heat. Cook turkey in skillet about 3 minutes on each side or until light brown.

3. Move turkey to one side of skillet. Add stir-fry sauce mixture and vegetables to other side of skillet; stir well to coat vegetables with sauce.

4. Heat to boiling; reduce heat to medium. Cover and cook 10 to 12 minutes, stirring occasionally, until vegetables are crisp-tender. Stir in orange wedges. Serve turkey topped with vegetable mixture.

1 Serving: Calories 265; Fat 11g; Cholesterol 70mg; Sodium 920mg; Carbohydrate 20g (Dietary Fiber 4g); Protein 25g

Fresh Fish and Vegetable Packets

4 servings

4 lean fish fillets (about 4 ounces each)

1 package (16 ounces) frozen broccoli, cauliflower and carrots, thawed

1 tablespoon chopped fresh or 1 teaspoon dried dill weed

1/2 teaspoon salt

1/4 teaspoon pepper

1/4 cup dry white wine or chicken broth

1. Heat oven to 450°.

2. Place each fish fillet on a 12-inch square of aluminum foil. Top each fish fillet with one-fourth of the vegetables. Sprinkle with dill weed, salt and pepper. Drizzle 1 tablespoon wine over each mound of vegetables.

3. Fold up sides of foil to make a tent; fold top edges over to seal. Fold in sides, making a packet; fold to seal. Place packets on ungreased cookie sheet.

4. Bake about 20 minutes or until vegetables are crisp-tender and fish flakes easily with fork.

1 Serving: Calories 130; Fat 2g; Cholesterol 60mg; Sodium 400mg; Carbohydrate 7g (Dietary Fiber 2g); Protein 23g

Grilled Garlic Halibut

4 servings

2 tablespoons olive or vegetable oil

1/4 teaspoon salt

1/8 teaspoon ground red pepper (cayenne)

1 clove garlic, finely chopped

4 halibut steaks, 1 inch thick (about 1 1/2 pounds)

Chopped fresh cilantro, if desired

1. Brush grill rack with vegetable oil. Heat coals or gas grill for direct heat.

2. Mix oil, salt, red pepper and garlic; spread on both sides of fish.

3. Cover and grill fish 4 to 6 inches from medium heat 10 to 15 minutes, turning once or until fish flakes easily with fork. Sprinkle with cilantro.

1 Serving: Calories 175; Fat 8g; Cholesterol 75mg; Sodium 260mg; Carbohydrate 0g (Dietary Fiber 0g); Protein 26g

112

Quick Red Snapper Teriyaki

4 servings

1 tablespoon vegetable oil

1 pound red snapper or other
  lean fish fillets, cut into
  1-inch pieces

3 cups 1-inch pieces asparagus

1 medium red bell pepper,
  cut into strips

1/2 cup teriyaki baste and glaze

Hot cooked noodles or rice,
  if desired

1. Heat wok or 12-inch skillet over medium-high heat. Add oil; rotate wok to coat side.

2. Add fish; stir-fry 2 minutes. Add asparagus and bell pepper; stir-fry 2 to 3 minutes or until vegetables are crisp-tender. Stir in teriyaki baste and glaze; cook 30 seconds or until hot. Serve with noodles.

1 Serving: Calories 185; Fat 5g; Cholesterol 60mg; Sodium 1480 mg; Carbohydrate 11g (Dietary Fiber 2g); Protein 26g

Tuna Spaghetti

4 servings

1 package (7 ounces) spaghetti

1/4 cup (1/2 stick) margarine,
butter or spread

2 cloves garlic, finely chopped

3/4 cup half-and-half

1 teaspoon dried basil leaves

1 can (9 1/4 ounces) tuna,
drained

1/2 cup sliced pimiento-stuffed
olives

1/4 cup grated Parmesan cheese

Chopped fresh parsley, if desired

1. Cook and drain spaghetti as directed on package.

2. While spaghetti is cooking, melt margarine in 2-quart saucepan over medium-high heat. Cook garlic in margarine, stirring occasionally, until golden. Stir in half-and-half and basil; heat to boiling.

3. Stir in tuna, olives and cheese; cook until hot. Serve over spaghetti. Sprinkle with parsley.

1 Serving: Calories 510; Fat 26g; Cholesterol 30mg; Sodium 890mg; Carbohydrate 43g (Dietary Fiber 1g); Protein 27g

114

Scampi with Fettuccine

4 servings

1 pound fresh or frozen raw
  medium shrimp (in shells)

6 ounces uncooked spinach
  fettuccine

2 tablespoons thinly sliced green
  onions

1 tablespoon chopped fresh or
  1 1/2 teaspoons dried basil
  leaves

1 tablespoon chopped fresh
  parsley

2 tablespoons lemon juice

1/4 teaspoon salt

2 cloves garlic, finely chopped

1. Peel shrimp. (If shrimp are frozen, do not thaw; peel in cold water.) Make a shallow cut lengthwise down back of each shrimp; wash out vein.

2. Cook and drain fettuccine as directed on package.

3. While fettuccine is cooking, spray 10-inch skillet with nonstick cooking spray; heat over medium heat. Add shrimp and remaining ingredients. Cook 2 to 3 minutes, stirring frequently, until shrimp are pink; remove from heat. Toss fettuccine and shrimp mixture in skillet.

1 Serving: Calories 195; Fat 2g; Cholesterol 145mg; Sodium 440mg; Carbohydrate 29g (Dietary Fiber 2g); Protein 17g

115

Lemony Seafood Risotto

4 servings

2 teaspoons olive or vegetable
oil

1/4 cup finely chopped shallots
(about 2 large) or green
onions

2 cloves garlic, finely chopped

1 cup uncooked arborio or
regular medium-grain
white rice

1/2 cup dry white wine or
nonalcoholic white wine

2 cans (14 1/2 ounces each)
1/3-less-salt clear chicken
broth

2 teaspoons olive or vegetable
oil

1/2 pound bay scallops

1/2 pound raw medium shrimp,
peeled and deveined

1 teaspoon grated lemon peel

2 tablespoons fresh chopped
parsley

1. Heat 2 teaspoons oil in 12-inch nonstick skillet over medium-high heat. Cook shallots and garlic in oil, stirring frequently, until shallots are crisp-tender. Reduce heat to medium. Stir in rice. Cook, stirring frequently, until rice begins to brown. Stir in wine. Cook until liquid is absorbed.

2. Pour 1/2 cup of the broth over rice mixture. Cook uncovered, stirring occasionally, until liquid is absorbed. Continue cooking 15 to 20 minutes, adding broth 1/2 cup at a time and stirring occasionally, until rice is tender and creamy.

3. Meanwhile, heat 2 teaspoons oil in 10-inch skillet over medium heat. Cook scallops and shrimp in oil 4 to 5 minutes, stirring frequently, until shrimp are pink and scallops are white. Remove scallops and shrimp from skillet, using slotted spoon. Gently stir scallops, shrimp and lemon peel into cooked rice mixture. Sprinkle with parsley.

1 Serving: Calories 305; Fat 6g; Cholesterol 70mg; Sodium 580mg; Carbohydrate 41g (Dietary Fiber 1g); Protein 23g

116

Savory Skillet Shrimp and Scallops

4 servings

1 pound fresh or frozen (thawed) medium shrimp, peeled and deveined

2 tablespoons olive or vegetable oil

1 clove garlic, finely chopped

1 green onion, chopped

1 medium green bell pepper, diced

1 tablespoon chopped fresh parsley or 1 teaspoon dried parsley flakes

1 pound sea scallops, cut in half

1/2 cup dry white wine or chicken broth

1 tablespoon lemon juice

1/4 to 1/2 teaspoon crushed red pepper

Hot cooked pasta, if desired

1. Heat oil in 10-inch skillet over medium heat. Cook garlic, onion, bell pepper and parsley in oil about 5 minutes, stirring occasionally, until bell pepper is crisp-tender. Stir in remaining ingredients.

2. Cook 4 to 5 minutes, stirring frequently, until shrimp are pink and scallops are white. Serve with pasta.

1 Serving: Calories 275; Fat 9g; Cholesterol 200mg; Sodium 490mg; Carbohydrate 6g (Dietary Fiber 3g); Protein 43g

118

Garlic Shrimp

4 servings

1 tablespoon vegetable oil

3 large cloves garlic, finely
chopped

1 pound uncooked medium
shrimp, peeled and deveined

1 large carrot, cut into julienne
strips (1 cup)

2 tablespoons chopped
fresh cilantro

Hot cooked noodles or rice,
if desired

1. Heat wok or 12-inch skillet over medium-high heat.
Add oil; rotate wok to coat side.

2. Add garlic; stir-fry 1 minute. Add shrimp; stir-fry
1 minute. Add carrot; stir-fry about 3 minutes or until
shrimp are pink and firm and carrot is crisp-tender.
Stir in cilantro. Serve over noodles.

1 Serving: Calories 120; Fat 4g; Cholesterol 160mg; Sodium 200mg;
Carbohydrate 4g (Dietary Fiber 1g); Protein 18g

120

Chapter 6

Easy Pasta, Grains and Beans

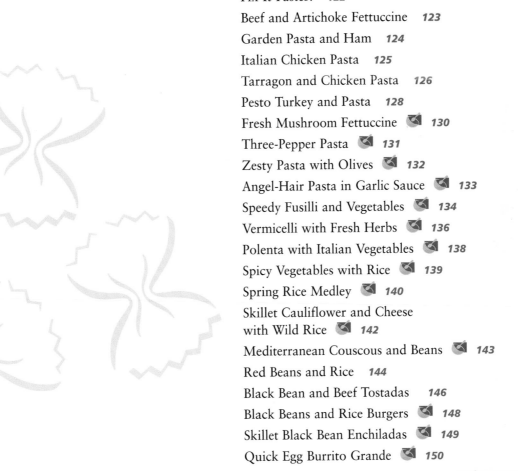

 meatless

Fix-It-Faster!

Fry leftover pasta and sprinkle with Parmesan cheese, chili powder, garlic salt, lemon pepper or your favorite spice.

Use prepared spaghetti sauce with cooked meat or sausage as a starting point for pasta.

To save time, freeze cooked pasta, grains and cooked beans. Thaw and add to the recipes calling for cooked pasta, grains and beans.

Save leftover rice for fried rice, or to serve with main dishes. It will save you from having to prepare it again. It also freezes well.

Create a bean burger by spreading buns with mayonnaise. Top with baked beans and cheese. Broil until cheese melts.

Use a rice mix and canned beans for a tasty rice-bean combination such as Spanish Rice and Beans.

Combine canned black-eye peas and cooked greens for a quick side dish.

Beef and Artichoke Fettuccine

6 servings

8 ounces uncooked fettuccine

1 jar (6 ounces) marinated
  artichoke hearts, cut in half
  and marinade reserved

1 small onion, finely chopped
  (1/4 cup)

1 cup half-and-half

1/2 cup grated Parmesan cheese

2 cups cut-up cooked roast beef

Coarsley ground black pepper,
  if desired

1. Cook and drain pasta as directed on package.

2. While pasta is cooking, heat 1 tablespoon reserved marinade to boiling in 10-inch skillet over medium heat. Discard remaining marinade. Cook onion in marinade about 4 minutes or until crisp-tender, stirring occasionally.

3. Stir in half-and-half; heat until hot. Stir in cheese, artichoke hearts and beef; heat until hot. Stir in fettuccine and toss. Sprinkle with pepper.

1 Serving: Calories 300; Fat 12g; Cholesterol 80mg; Sodium 260mg; Carbohydrate 31g (Dietary Fiber 3g); Protein 20g

123

Garden Pasta and Ham

4 servings

2 cups uncooked penne or
   mostaccioli pasta (7 ounces)

1 cup sliced zucchini

1 cup sliced yellow summer
   squash

2 cups cubed fully cooked
   smoked ham

1/2 cup reduced-fat Italian
   dressing

1/4 cup chopped fresh basil
   leaves

1/3 cup shredded Parmesan
   cheese

Coarsely ground black pepper,
   if desired

1. Cook penne as directed on package except during last
3 to 4 minutes of cooking, add zucchini and squash to
pasta; drain.

2. Return pasta mixture to saucepan; add ham, dressing
and basil. Cook over medium heat until hot, stirring
occasionally. Sprinkle with Parmesan cheese and pepper.

1 Serving: Calories 505; Fat 16g; Cholesterol 65mg; Sodium 400mg;
Carbohydrate 57g (Dietary Fiber 4g); Protein 37g

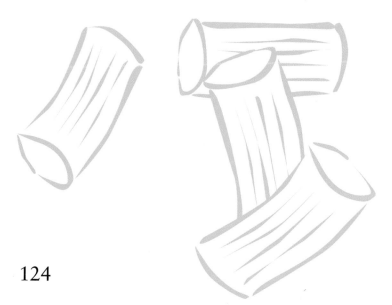

124

Italian Chicken Pasta

6 servings

8 ounces uncooked spaghetti

1 pound asparagus, cut into 2-inch pieces

8 sun-dried tomatoes (not oil-packed), chopped

2 cloves garlic, finely chopped

1 1/2 cups chopped yellow bell pepper

3/4 cup chopped red onion

2 cups chicken broth

1 1/2 pounds boneless, skinless chicken breast halves, cut into 1/2-inch strips

3/4 cup nonfat ricotta cheese

1/3 cup chopped fresh basil leaves

2 tablespoons low-fat sour cream

1/2 teaspoon salt

1/4 teaspoon pepper

1. Cook spaghetti as directed on package; drain.

2. Cook asparagus, tomatoes, garlic, bell pepper and onion in broth in 10-inch skillet over medium heat 5 minutes. Stir in chicken. Cook 2 to 3 minutes, stirring constantly, until asparagus is crisp-tender and chicken is no longer pink in center.

3. Stir in spaghetti and remaining ingredients. Toss about 30 seconds or until heated through.

1 Serving: Calories 370; Fat 7g; Cholesterol 75mg; Sodium 540mg; Carbohydrate 40g (Dietary Fiber 3g); Protein 37g

125

Tarragon and Chicken Pasta

4 servings

1 1/2 cups uncooked mostaccioli
pasta (4 1/2 ounces)

2 cups sliced mushrooms
(6 ounces)

1 cup broccoli flowerets

2 medium carrots, thinly sliced
(1 cup)

1 cup skim milk

1 tablespoon cornstarch

2 teaspoons chopped fresh or
1/2 teaspoon dried tarragon
leaves

1/4 teaspoon salt

1 clove garlic, finely chopped

2 cups shredded spinach or
romaine (2 1/2 ounces)

1 1/2 cups cut-up cooked
chicken or turkey

1/2 cup shredded reduced-fat
Swiss cheese (2 ounces)

1. Cook pasta as directed on package in 3-quart saucepan, adding mushrooms, broccoli and carrots the last 4 minutes of cooking

2. While pasta is cooking, mix milk, cornstarch, tarragon, salt and garlic in 1 1/2-quart saucepan. Cook over medium heat, stirring constantly, until mixture thickens and boils. Stir in remaining ingredients until cheese is melted and spinach is wilted.

3. Drain pasta mixture; toss with sauce.

1 Serving: Calories 360; Fat 6g; Cholesterol 45mg; Sodium 280mg; Carbohydrate 51g (Dietary Fiber 4g); Protein 30g

Pesto Turkey and Pasta

4 servings

3 cups uncooked farfalle
(bow-tie) pasta (6 ounces)

2 cups cubed cooked turkey
breast

1/2 cup pesto

1/2 cup coarsely chopped
roasted red bell peppers

Sliced ripe olives, if desired

1. Cook pasta as directed on package in 3-quart saucepan. Drain.

2. Mix hot cooked pasta, turkey, pesto and bell peppers in same saucepan. Heat over low heat, stirring constantly, until hot. Garnish with olives.

1 Serving: Calories 460; Fat 23g; Cholesterol 55mg; Sodium 160mg; Carbohydrate 36g (Dietary Fiber 2g); Protein 29g

Fresh Mushroom Fettuccine

8 servings

8 ounces uncooked fettuccine

3 cups sliced mushrooms (about 8 ounces)

1/4 cup chopped fresh parsley

1/4 cup red wine vinegar

1/4 cup olive or vegetable oil

3 tablespoons freshly grated Parmesan cheese

2 teaspoons chopped fresh rosemary leaves

1/2 teaspoon freshly ground pepper

1/4 teaspoon salt

1 clove garlic, crushed

1. Cook and drain fettuccine as directed on package. Rinse with cold water; drain.

2. Toss fettuccine and remaining ingredients.

1 Serving: Calories 175; Fat 9g; Cholesterol 25mg; Sodium 230mg; Carbohydrate 21g (Dietary Fiber 2g); Protein 5g

Three-Pepper Pasta

6 servings

3 cups uncooked farfalle (bow tie) pasta (about 8 ounces)

1 tablespoon olive or vegetable oil

1 small green bell pepper, cut into 1/4-inch strips

1 small red bell pepper, cut into 1/4-inch strips

1 small yellow bell pepper, cut into 1/4-inch strips

1 cup purchased spaghetti sauce

Chopped fresh basil, if desired

Shredded Parmesan cheese, if desired

1. Cook and drain pasta as directed on package.

2. While pasta is cooking, heat oil in 10-inch non-stick skillet over medium heat. Cook bell peppers in oil about 5 minutes, stirring occasionally, until crisp-tender. Stir in spaghetti sauce. Cook until heated through.

3. Serve over pasta. Sprinkle with basil and Parmesan cheese.

1 Serving: Calories 105; Fat 3g; Cholesterol 0mg; Sodium 200mg; Carbohydrate 18g (Dietary Fiber 2g); Protein 3g

131

Zesty Pasta with Olives

4 servings

4 cups uncooked rotini pasta
  (about 8 ounces)

2 tablespoons olive or vegetable
  oil

3 tablespoons red wine vinegar

2 tablespoons chopped fresh or
  1 1/2 teaspoons dried
  oregano leaves

1/4 teaspoon salt

1/4 to 1/2 teaspoon crushed
  red pepper

2 cloves garlic, crushed

2 tablespoons sliced pimiento-
  stuffed olives

2 tablespoons sliced ripe olives

2 cups broccoli flowerets

2 medium zucchini, cut into
  1/4-inch slices (about 2 cups)

1. Cook and drain pasta as directed on package.

2. While pasta is cooking, heat oil, vinegar, oregano, salt, red pepper and garlic in 10-inch nonstick skillet. Cook olives, broccoli and zucchini in oil mixture, stirring occasionally, until broccoli is crisp-tender. Serve over pasta.

1 Serving: Calories 300; Fat 10g; Cholesterol 0mg; Sodium 550mg; Carbohydrate 48g (Dietary Fiber 7g); Protein 11g

Angel-Hair Pasta in Garlic Sauce

6 servings

1 *package (16 ounces) capellini (angel-hair) pasta*

1/4 *cup olive or vegetable oil*

1/4 *cup chopped fresh parsley*

4 *cloves garlic, finely chopped*

1/2 *cup freshly grated Parmesan cheese*

Freshly ground pepper

1. Cook pasta as directed on package; drain.

2. Meanwhile, heat oil in 10-inch skillet over medium-high heat. Cook parsley and garlic in oil, stirring frequently, until garlic is soft.

3. Toss pasta with garlic mixture. Sprinkle with cheese. Serve with pepper.

1 Serving: Calories 400; Fat 12g; Cholesterol 5mg; Sodium 430mg; Carbohydrate 62g (Dietary Fiber 1g); Protein 13g

133

Speedy Fusilli and Vegetables

6 servings

1 package (12 ounces) tricolored corkscrew (fusilli) pasta

1 tablespoon olive or vegetable oil

1 tablespoon chopped fresh or 1 teaspoon dried basil leaves

1 teaspoon freshly ground pepper

2 cups julienne strips carrots (about 4 medium)

1 medium yellow bell pepper, cut into 2-inch strips

1 can (15 to 16 ounces) cannellini beans, rinsed and drained

1 can (15 ounces) tomato sauce with tomato bits

1 can (14 ounces) artichoke hearts, drained and cut into fourths

1/2 cup freshly grated Parmesan cheese or shredded farmer cheese

1. Cook pasta as directed on package; drain.

2. Heat oil in 12-inch skillet over medium-high heat. Cook basil, pepper, carrots and bell pepper in oil about 3 minutes, stirring occasionally, until carrots are crisp-tender.

3. Stir in pasta, beans, tomato sauce and artichoke hearts. Cook about 5 minutes, stirring occasionally, until hot. Sprinkle with cheese.

1 Serving: Calories 480; Fat 8g; Cholesterol 5mg; Sodium 1130mg; Carbohydrate 90g (Dietary Fiber 8g); Protein 20g

134

Vermicelli with Fresh Herbs

6 servings

1 package (16 ounces) vermicelli

1/4 cup olive or vegetable oil

2 tablespoons pine nuts

1 tablespoon chopped fresh
   parsley

1 tablespoon capers

2 teaspoons chopped fresh
   rosemary leaves

2 teaspoons chopped fresh
   sage leaves

1 teaspoon chopped fresh
   basil leaves

1 pint cherry tomatoes, cut into
   fourths

Freshly ground pepper

1. Cook vermicelli as directed on package; drain.

2. Meanwhile, mix oil, pine nuts, parsley, capers, rosemary, sage and basil in medium bowl. Stir in tomatoes.

3. Toss vermicelli and herb mixture. Serve with pepper.

1 Serving: Calories 395; Fat 12g; Cholesterol 0mg; Sodium 310mg; Carbohydrate 64g (Dietary Fiber 2g); Protein 11g

Polenta with Italian Vegetables

6 servings

1 cup yellow cornmeal

3/4 cup cold water

2 1/2 cups boiling water

1/2 teaspoon salt

2/3 cup shredded Swiss cheese
(about 2 1/2 ounces)

2 cups sliced yellow squash

1 cup sliced zucchini

1 cup chopped red bell pepper

1/4 cup finely chopped onion

1 clove garlic, crushed

2 teaspoons olive or vegetable
oil

1/4 cup chopped fresh or
1 tablespoon dried basil
leaves

1 can (14 ounces) artichoke
hearts, drained and cut into
fourths

1. Mix cornmeal and cold water in 2-quart saucepan. Stir in boiling water and salt. Cook, stirring constantly, until mixture thickens and boils; reduce heat. Cover and cook 10 minutes, stirring occasionally. Add cheese and stir until smooth; keep polenta warm.

2. Cook squash, zucchini, bell pepper, onion and garlic in oil in 10-inch skillet over medium-high heat about 5 minutes, stirring occasionally, until vegetables are crisp-tender. Stir in basil and artichokes. Spoon polenta into shallow platter; top with vegetable mixture.

1 Serving: Calories 190; Fat 6g; Cholesterol 10mg; Sodium 260mg; Carbohydrate 31g (Dietary Fiber 5g); Protein 8g

Spicy Vegetables with Rice

6 servings

1 tablespoon vegetable oil

1/4 cup chopped green onions

1/2 teaspoon ground ginger

4 cloves garlic, crushed

1/4 cup chicken broth

1 teaspoon curry powder

1/2 teaspoon salt

1/8 teaspoon ground red pepper (cayenne)

1 1/4 cups chopped zucchini (about 2 small)

1 small eggplant (about 1 pound), cut into 1-inch pieces

1 small red bell pepper, thinly sliced

1 small green bell pepper, thinly sliced

2 cans (15 to 16 ounces each) cannellini beans, rinsed and drained

3 cups hot cooked rice

1. Heat oil in 10-inch skillet over medium-high heat. Cook onions, ginger and garlic in oil 2 minutes, stirring occasionally. Stir in remaining ingredients except beans and rice.

2. Cook about 5 minutes, stirring frequently, until vegetables are crisp-tender. Stir in beans. Cook until thoroughly heated. Serve with rice.

1 Serving: Calories 270; Fat 3g; Cholesterol 0mg; Sodium 840mg; Carbohydrate 59g (Dietary Fiber 10g); Protein 12g

139

Spring Rice Medley

6 servings

1 pound asparagus, cut into
2-inch pieces

3 cups broccoli flowerets

2 teaspoons olive or vegetable
oil

1 medium red bell pepper cut
into 1/4-inch strips

1 medium zucchini, sliced

1 medium onion, chopped

4 cups cooked rice

2 cups coarsely chopped seeded
tomatoes (about 2 large)

3/4 teaspoon salt

1/2 teaspoon saffron threads or
1/4 teaspoon ground turmeric

2 cans (15 to 16 ounces each)
garbanzo beans, rinsed and
drained

1 package (10 ounces) frozen
green peas, thawed

1. Cook asparagus and broccoli in enough boiling water
to cover in 2-quart saucepan about 4 minutes or until
crisp-tender; drain.

2. Heat oil in Dutch oven over medium-high heat. Cook
asparagus, broccoli, bell pepper, zucchini and onion in
oil about 5 minutes, stirring occasionally, until onion
is crisp-tender. Stir in remaining ingredients. Cook
about 5 minutes, stirring frequently, until hot.

1 Serving: Calories 280; Fat 4g; Cholesterol 0mg; Sodium 640mg;
Carbohydrate 58g (Dietary Fiber 10g); Protein 13g

Skillet Cauliflower and Cheese with Wild Rice

4 servings

1 can (14 1/2 ounces) ready-to-serve vegetable broth

2 tablespoons margarine or butter

1 package (16 ounces) frozen cauliflower, carrots and asparagus

1 package (6.2 ounces) long grain and wild rice fast-cooking mix

3/4 cup shredded Cheddar cheese (3 ounces)

1. Heat broth and margarine to boiling in 10-inch skillet. Stir in vegetables, rice and contents of seasoning packet. Heat to boiling; reduce heat to low.

2. Cover and simmer 5 to 6 minutes or until vegetables and rice are tender. Sprinkle with cheese.

1 Serving: Calories 315; Fat 13g; Cholesterol 20mg; Sodium 1540mg; Carbohydrate 40g (Dietary Fiber 4g); Protein 13g

Mediterranean Couscous and Beans

4 servings

3 cups chicken broth

2 cups uncooked couscous

1/2 cup raisins or currants

1/4 teaspoon pepper

1/8 teaspoon ground red pepper
(cayenne)

1 small tomato, chopped
(1/2 cup)

1 can (15 to 16 ounces) garbanzo
beans, rinsed and drained

1/3 cup crumbled feta cheese

1. Heat broth to boiling in 3-quart saucepan. Stir in remaining ingredients except cheese; remove from heat.

2. Cover and let stand about 5 minutes or until liquid is absorbed; stir gently. Sprinkle each serving with cheese.

1 Serving: Calories 540; Fat 6g; Cholesterol 10mg; Sodium 620mg; Carbohydrate 108g (Dietary Fiber 9g); Protein 22

143

Red Beans and Rice

4 servings

1 package (4 1/2 ounces) Cajun-style rice and sauce mix.

2 cups water

2 fully cooked spicy smoked sausage links (2 1/2 to 3 ounces), thinly sliced (from 16 ounce package)

1 can (15 to 16 ounces) kidney beans, rinsed and drained

1. Heat rice and sauce mix, water and sausage to boiling in 2-quart saucepan; reduce heat to low.

2. Cook uncovered about 10 minutes, stirring occasionally, until rice is tender. Stir in beans; heat 1 minute.

1 Serving: Calories 295; Fat 10g; Cholesterol 25mg; Sodium 1100mg; Carbohydrate 40g (Dietary Fiber 5g); Protein 16g

144

Black Bean and Beef Tostadas

6 servings

1/2 pound ground beef

1 medium onion, chopped (1/2 cup)

1 can (10 ounces) chopped tomatoes and green chilies, undrained

1 can (15 ounces) black beans, rinsed and drained

6 tostada shells

1 cup shredded lettuce

2/3 cup chopped tomato

3/4 cup shredded Colby-Monterey Jack cheese (3 ounces)

1. Cook beef and onion in 10-inch skillet over medium-high heat, stirring occasionally, until beef is brown; drain.

2. Stir in tomatoes. Heat to boiling; reduce heat to low. Simmer uncovered about 10 minutes or until liquid has evaporated. Stir in beans.

3. Heat tostada shells as directed on package. Top tostada shells with bean mixture, lettuce, tomato and cheese.

1 Serving: Calories 360; Fat 14g; Cholesterol 35mg; Sodium 530mg; Carbohydrate 44g (Dietary Fiber 6g); Protein 20g

Black Beans and Rice Burgers

4 servings

1 can (15 to 16 ounces) black
    beans, rinsed and drained

1 cup cooked rice

1 small onion, finely chopped
    (1/4 cup)

2 tablespoons salsa

1/4 cup sour cream

1/4 cup salsa

4 hamburger buns, split

Lettuce leaves

1. Mash beans. Mix beans, rice, onion and 2 tablespoons salsa.

2. Spray 10-inch skillet with nonstick cooking spray; heat over medium-high heat. Spoon bean mixture by 1/2 cupfuls into skillet; flatten to 1/2 inch. Cook 4 to 5 minutes on each side or until light brown. Remove patties from skillet. Cover and keep warm while cooking remaining patties.

3. Mix sour cream and 1/4 cup salsa; spread on buns. Top with burgers and lettuce.

1 Serving: Calories 320; Fat 6g; Cholesterol 10mg; Sodium 620mg; Carbohydrate 61g (Dietary Fiber 9g); Protein 14g

Skillet Black Bean Enchiladas

4 servings

1 teaspoon vegetable oil

1 medium onion, chopped
(1/2 cup)

1 clove garlic, finely chopped

1 cup sour cream

1 tablespoon lime juice

1/2 teaspoon ground cumin

2 cans (15 ounces each) black
beans, rinsed, drained and
mashed

10 flour tortillas (8 to 10 inches
in diameter)

1 can (15 ounces) tomato sauce

1/2 cup shredded Monterey Jack
cheese with jalapeño peppers

1. Heat oil in 10-inch skillet over medium-high heat. Cook onion and garlic in oil about 2 minutes, stirring occasionally, until onion is crisp-tender. Stir in sour cream, lime juice, cumin and beans. Remove mixture from skillet.

2. Spoon about 1/3 cup bean mixture onto each tortilla. Roll tortilla around filling; place seam side down in skillet. Pour tomato sauce over tortillas. Sprinkle with cheese. Cook over low heat 10 to 15 minutes or until hot and bubbly.

1 Serving: Calories 480; Fat 16g; Cholesterol 40mg; Sodium 1260mg; Carbohydrate 77g (Dietary Fiber 16g); Protein 23g

Quick Egg Burrito Grande

4 servings

1 cup diced potato
  (about 1 medium)

1 cup chopped green bell pepper
  (about 1 medium)

1/4 cup chopped onion
  (about 1 small)

1/2 teaspoon chili powder

1 teaspoon margarine or butter

5 eggs, slightly beaten

1 cup canned refried beans,
  heated

1/2 cup shredded reduced-fat
  or regular Cheddar cheese
  (2 ounces)

1/2 cup chopped seeded tomato
  (about 1 small)

1/2 cup salsa

8 flour tortillas (8 to 10 inches
  in diameter)

1. Spray 10-inch skillet with nonstick cooking spray. Cook potato, bell pepper and onion in skillet over medium heat, stirring occasionally, until tender. Stir in chili powder. Remove from skillet; keep warm.

2. Heat margarine in same skillet over medium heat until melted. Cook eggs in margarine, stirring frequently, until set but still moist.

3. For each burrito, spread about 2 tablespoons beans, 2 tablespoons potato mixture, 1 tablespoon cheese, 2 tablespoons eggs, 1 tablespoon tomato and 1 table-spoon salsa in center of each tortilla. Fold tortilla around filling.

1 Serving: Calories 510; Fat 17g; Cholesterol 280mg; Sodium 1070mg; Carbohydrate 73g (Dietary Fiber 7g); Protein 23g

Chapter 7

On the Side

Fix-It-Faster!

Purchase cut-up vegetables from your deli, salad bar, or produce section to cut down on prep work.

Grill or bake whole or mixed cut-up vegetables in foil packages. Top with margarine or butter and your favorite herb.

Use leftover potatoes for hash browns or in potato salad.

Toss cooked vegetables with melted margarine or olive oil and salad dressing mix.

Stir salad dressing mix (ranch-style) into mashed potatoes for a real flavor treat.

Create a quick sauce to serve with hot or cold vegetables. Try salsa or jarred or soft cheese spread thinned with milk or beer.

Toss hot cooked vegetables with soy sauce, teriyaki sauce, chili sauce, barbecue sauce or sweet-and-sour sauce, or your favorite, for a new twist on vegetables.

Summer Squash Sauté

4 servings

1 teaspoon olive or vegetable oil

1/2 cup chopped red onion

1 clove garlic, finely chopped

2 1/2 cups coarsely chopped or sliced yellow summer squash or zucchini

1 tablespoon balsamic or white wine vinegar

1 1/2 cups coarsely chopped tomatoes (about 2 medium)

2 tablespoons chopped fresh basil leaves

1/8 teaspoon salt

Dash of pepper

1. Heat oil in 8-inch skillet over medium heat.

2. Cook onion and garlic in oil about 2 minutes, stirring occasionally, until onion is tender. Stir in squash and balsamic vinegar. Cook about 3 minutes, stirring occasionally, until squash is crisp-tender. Stir in tomatoes. Cook about 2 minutes, stirring frequently, until tomatoes are heated through.

3. Stir in remaining ingredients.

1 Serving: Calories 50; Fat 2g; Cholesterol 0mg; Sodium 80mg; Carbohydrate 8g (Dietary Fiber 2g); Protein 2g

153

Asparagus with Honey Mustard

2 servings

12 to 16 spears asparagus

3 tablespoons honey

2 tablespoons Dijon Mustard

4 teaspoons lemon juice

2 teaspoons olive or vegetable oil

1. Snap off tough ends of asparagus spears. Heat 1 inch water (salted if desired) to boiling in 10-inch skillet; add asparagus. Heat to boiling. Cover and cook 8 to 12 minutes or until stalk ends are crisp-tender; drain.

2. Shake remaining ingredients in tightly covered container. Drizzle dressing over asparagus.

1 Serving: Calories 185; Fat 6g; Cholesterol 0mg; Sodium 190mg; Carbohydrate 32g (Dietary Fiber 2g); Protein 3g

154

Southwest Vegetable Sauté

8 servings

1/4 cup (1/2 stick) margarine or
butter

1 medium onion, finely chopped

2 cloves garlic, finely chopped

4 very small pattypan squash
(about 4 ounces each),
cut in half

2 medium zucchini, cut into
1/4-inch strips

2 medium yellow summer
squash, cut into 1/4-inch
slices

1 small red bell pepper, cut into
thin rings

1 small yellow bell pepper,
cut into thin rings

1/2 teaspoon salt

1/4 teaspoon ground red pepper
(cayenne)

Margarine or butter, melted,
if desired

Grated lime peel, if desired

1. Melt 1/4 cup margarine in 12-inch skillet over medium-high heat. Cook onion and garlic in margarine, stirring occasionally, until onion is tender.

2. Stir in remaining ingredients except melted margarine. Cook over medium-high heat, stirring occasionally, until vegetables are crisp-tender. Drizzle with melted margarine, and sprinkle with lime peel.

1 Serving: Calories 80; Fat 6g; Cholesterol 0mg; Sodium 200mg; Carbohydrate 7g (Dietary Fiber 2g); Protein 1g

155

Pesto Vegetables

5 servings

1 package (16 ounces) frozen broccoli, cauliflower and carrots

1/3 cup pesto

2 tablespoons grated Parmesan cheese

1. Cook and drain vegetables as directed on package.

2. Toss vegetables and pesto. Sprinkle with cheese.

1 Serving: Calories 135; Fat 11g; Cholesterol 5mg; Sodium 125mg; Carbohydrate 7g (Dietary Fiber 2g); Protein 4g

Caesar Vegetable Medley

6 servings

2 tablespoons olive or vegetable oil

2 packages (16 ounces each) frozen cauliflower, carrots and snow pea pods

1 envelope (1.2 ounces) Caesar salad dressing mix

1. Heat oil in 10-inch nonstick skillet over medium-high heat.

2. Add vegetables and dressing mix to oil. Cover and cook 5 to 7 minutes, stirring frequently until vegetables are crisp-tender.

1 Serving: Calories 115; Fat 5g; Cholesterol 0mg; Sodium 450mg; Carbohydrate 13g (Dietary Fiber 0g); Protein 4g

Garden Salad with Honey French Dressing

4 servings

6 cups bite-size pieces romaine
    or red leaf lettuce

2/3 cup chopped peeled cucumber
    (about 1/2 medium)

3/4 cup chopped tomato
    (about 1 medium)

1/4 cup chopped red onion

1/4 cup raisins

2 tablespoons sunflower nuts

2 ounces blue cheese, crumbled,
    if desired

Honey French Dressing (right)

1. Toss lettuce, cucumber, tomato and onion in large salad bowl. Sprinkle with raisins, sunflower nuts and cheese.

2. Serve with Honey French Dressing.

HONEY FRENCH DRESSING

1/3 cup ketchup

3 tablespoons seasoned rice vinegar

2 tablespoons honey

1 tablespoon vegetable oil

1 tablespoon water

Shake all ingredients in tightly covered container.

1 Serving: Calories 175; Fat 6g; Cholesterol 0mg; Sodium 240mg; Carbohydrate 27g (Dietary Fiber 2g); Protein 4g

159

Honey-Lime Fruit Salad

4 servings

1/2 cup honey

1/4 cup frozen limeade
concentrate, thawed

2 teaspoons poppy seeds,
if desired

4 cups cut-up fresh fruit

1/4 cup slivered almonds,
toasted

1. Mix honey, limeade concentrate and poppy seeds in medium bowl.

2. Carefully toss fruit with honey mixture. Sprinkle with almonds.

1 Serving: Calories 270; Fat 8g; Cholesterol 0mg; Sodium 10mg; Carbohydrate 50g (Dietary Fiber 4g); Protein 4g

160

Fresh Melon Salad

6 servings

2 cups watermelon balls or cubes

2 mangoes or papayas, peeled, seeded and sliced

1/2 honeydew melon, peeled, seeded and thinly sliced

3/4 cup seedless red grapes

Lettuce leaves

Honey-Lime Dressing (right)

Arrange fruits on lettuce leaves. Drizzle with Honey-Lime Dressing.

HONEY-LIME DRESSING

1/4 cup vegetable oil

1/4 teaspoon grated lime peel

2 tablespoons lime juice

1 tablespoon honey

Shake all ingredients in tightly covered container.

1 Serving: Calories 215; Fat 10g; Cholesterol 0mg; Sodium 15mg; Carbohydrate 33g (Dietary Fiber 3g); Protein 1g

162

Lemon-Curry Rice

6 servings

2 cups chicken broth

2 tablespoons lemon juice

*1 cup uncooked regular long
grain rice*

1 teaspoon grated lemon peel

1/2 teaspoon curry powder

1/4 teaspoon garlic salt

1/8 teaspoon pepper

*2 tablespoons sliced almonds,
toasted*

1. Heat broth, lemon juice and rice to boiling in 2-quart saucepan; reduce heat to low. Cover and simmer 15 minutes (do not lift cover or stir); remove from heat.

2. Stir in lemon peel, curry powder, garlic salt and pepper.

3. Cover and let stand 10 minutes. Fluff rice lightly with fork. Sprinkle with almonds.

1 Serving: Calories 145; Fat 2g; Cholesterol 0mg; Sodium 320mg; Carbohydrate 28g (Dietary Fiber 1g); Protein 5g

Ginger Couscous with Apple

4 servings

3 cups hot water

1 tablespoon reduced-sodium chicken bouillon granules

1/8 teaspoon ground ginger

1 medium onion, thinly sliced

1 medium green bell pepper, chopped (1 cup)

1 cup uncooked couscous

1 medium unpeeled apple, coarsely chopped (1 cup)

1. Spray 10-inch nonstick skillet with cooking spray. Mix hot water, bouillon granules and ginger; set aside.

2. Cook onion and bell pepper in skillet over medium heat about 5 minutes, stirring occasionally, until onion is crisp-tender. Stir in couscous and water mixture. Heat to boiling; remove from heat.

3. Cover and let stand 5 minutes or until liquid is absorbed. Stir in apple.

1 Serving: Calories 205 (Calories from Fat 10); Fat 1g (Saturated 0g); Cholesterol 0mg; Sodium 10mg; Carbohydrate 46g (Dietary Fiber 4g); Protein 7g

Spinach Orzo

8 servings

2 teaspoons margarine

2 cloves garlic, finely chopped

1/2 cup coarsely shredded carrot

4 cups chicken broth

2 cups uncooked rosamarina
(orzo) pasta

1 package (10 ounces) frozen
chopped spinach, thawed and
squeezed to drain

1/2 cup grated Parmesan cheese

1 teaspoon dried basil leaves

Salt and pepper to taste

1. Melt margarine in 2-quart saucepan over medium heat. Cook garlic and carrot in margarine 2 minutes, stirring occasionally, until carrot is tender. Stir in broth, pasta and spinach. Heat to boiling; reduce heat.

2. Simmer 15 to 20 minutes or until broth is absorbed. Stir in remaining ingredients before serving.

1 Serving: Calories 180; Fat 4g; Cholesterol 5mg; Sodium 650mg; Carbohydrate 28g (Dietary Fiber 1g); Protein 9g

Chapter 8

Simply Delicious Desserts

Fix-It-Faster!

Use leftover muffins or popovers for dessert
by filling with pudding or ice cream and topping with
fresh fruit or your favorite dessert topping.

For a fast dessert using leftover cake: cube or
coarsely crumble the cake. Layer with fresh fruit, pudding,
ice cream and/or whipped cream.

Mix crumbled cake with pudding and serve in
ice cream cones—great for kids.

Brush pound cake or angel food cake slices with
melted margarine or butter. Roll in coconut or nuts and
brown both sides until golden.

Cut pound cake or sponge cake into fingers.
Dip into a glaze (heated ready-to-spread frosting
makes a good one), then roll into nuts, coconut, grated
chocolate, granola or chopped candy.

Use refrigerator cookie dough to make individual tarts.

Fold your favorite crumbled cookies into
sweetened whipped cream or yogurt. Serve over
fresh fruit, pound cake or brownies.

Make homemade cookie sandwiches by putting two
cookies or graham crackers together with your favorite
frosting, jam, peanut butter or cream cheese.

Raspberry-Chocolate Cream

4 servings

1 container (8 ounces) frozen
   whipped topping, thawed

1/2 cup chocolate-flavored
   syrup

1 pint raspberries

1. Layer 1/2 of whipped topping, 1 tablespoon syrup and 1/8 of raspberries in each of 4 dessert dishes.

2. Repeat with remaining ingredients.

1 Serving: Calories 200; Fat 13g; Cholesterol 0mg; Sodium 45mg; Carbohydrate 22g (Dietary Fiber 2g); Protein 1g

Creamy Caramel-Peach Parfaits

6 servings

2/3 cup caramel ice-cream topping

1 container (8 ounces) frozen whipped topping, thawed

1 can (29 ounces) sliced peaches, drained and cut into pieces

Molasses cookie crumbs, if desired

1. Fold ice-cream topping into whipped topping in small bowl.

2. Layer cookies, whipped topping mixture and peaches in 6 parfait or other tall glasses. Sprinkle with cookie crumbs. Serve immediately, or refrigerate until serving time.

1 Serving: Calories 370; Fat 12g; Cholesterol 0mg; Sodium 170mg; Carbohydrate 66g (Dietary Fiber 2g); Protein 2g

Angel Food–Coconut Cream Cake

12 servings

1 purchased round angel food cake (8 or 9 inches in diameter)

1 can (21 ounces) coconut pie filling

1 container (8 ounces) frozen whipped topping, thawed

2 tablespoons coconut, lightly toasted

1. Split cake horizontally to make 4 layers. (To split, mark side of cake with toothpicks and cut with long thin serrated knife.)

2. Place bottom layer on serving plate; spread with 1/3 cup of the pie filling. Repeat with 2 more layers. Replace top cake layer.

3. Frost top and sides of cake with whipped topping. Sprinkle top with coconut. Store in refrigerator.

1 Serving: Calories 260; Fat 10g; Cholesterol 50mg; Sodium 170mg; Carbohydrate 38g (Dietary Fiber 0g); Protein 4g

171

Quick Praline Bars

2 dozen bars

24 graham cracker squares

1/2 cup packed brown sugar

1/2 cup (1 stick) margarine or butter

1/2 teaspoon vanilla

1/2 cup chopped pecans

1. Heat oven to 350°.

2. Arrange graham crackers in single layer in ungreased jelly roll pan. 15 1/2 × 10 1/2 × 1 inch.

3. Heat brown sugar and margarine to boiling in 2-quart saucepan. Boil 1 minute, stirring constantly; remove from heat. Stir in vanilla.

4. Pour sugar mixture over crackers; spread evenly. Sprinkle with pecans. Bake 8 to 10 minutes or until bubbly; cool slightly.

1 Bar: Calories 90; Fat 6g; Cholesterol 0mg; Sodium 90mg; Carbohydrate 10g (Dietary Fiber 0g); Protein 0g.

Speedy Rice and Raisin Pudding

4 servings

1 cup uncooked instant rice

1 cup milk or water

1/4 cup raisins

3 tablespoons sugar

1/4 teaspoon salt

1/4 teaspoon ground cinnamon
    or nutmeg

1. Mix all ingredients in 2-quart saucepan. Heat to boiling, stirring constantly; remove from heat.

2. Cover and let stand 5 minutes.

1 Serving: Calories 195; Fat 1g; Cholesterol 5mg; Sodium 170mg; Carbohydrate 43g (Dietary Fiber 0g); Protein 4g

Toasty Chocolate and Banana Wrap

6 servings

3 firm, ripe medium bananas

2 tablespoons lemon juice

6 flour tortillas (8 or 10 inches in diameter)

1/4 cup sugar

3/4 teaspoon ground cinnamon

2 tablespoons margarine or butter, melted

1/3 cup chocolate, butterscotch or caramel ice-cream topping

1. Heat oven to 450°. Grease cookie sheet.

2. Peel bananas and cut lengthwise in half; brush with lemon juice. Place 1 banana half on each tortilla. Mix sugar and cinnamon, reserving 1 tablespoon. Sprinkle bananas with sugar and cinnamon. Roll each tortilla around banana; place seam side down on cookie sheet. Brush with margarine. Sprinkle with reserved sugar and cinnamon.

3. Bake 6 to 8 minutes or until golden brown. Place on dessert plates. Drizzle with ice-cream topping. Serve with ice cream, if desired.

1 Serving: Calories 295; Fat 7g; Cholesterol 0mg; Sodium 270mg; Carbohydrate 56g (Dietary Fiber 2g): Protein 4g

174

Brown Sugar Strawberries

4 servings

2 cups fresh strawberries

1/3 cup plain nonfat yogurt

1/3 cup loosely packed brown
   sugar

1. Rinse and dry strawberries, but do not hull. Place strawberries in serving bowl.

2. Place yogurt and brown sugar in 2 separate bowls.

3. To eat, dip strawberries into yogurt, and then into brown sugar.

1 Serving: Calories 95; Fat 0g; Cholesterol 0mg; Sodium 25mg; Carbohydrate 24g (Dietary Fiber 1g); Protein 1g

Apple-Raspberry Crisp

2 servings

1 1/2 cups chopped peeled
   cooking apples (about 2 small)

1/2 cup fresh or frozen
   raspberries, strawberries
   or blackberries

1 tablespoon granulated sugar

2 tablespoons brown sugar

3 tablespoons old-fashioned
   oats

1 tablespoon all-purpose flour

1/4 teaspoon ground cinnamon

1/8 teaspoon ground nutmeg

1 tablespoon margarine

1 teaspoon water

Vanilla low-fat frozen yogurt,
   if desired

1. Heat oven to 375°. Spray two 10-ounce custard cups or individual soufflé dishes with nonstick cooking spray.

2. Mix apples, raspberries and granulated sugar. Divide between custard cups.

3. Mix brown sugar, oats, flour, cinnamon and nutmeg in small bowl. Cut in margarine until crumbly. Spoon over apple mixture.

4. Bake about 25 minutes or until apples are tender and topping is golden. Serve warm with frozen yogurt.

1 Serving: Calories 260; Fat 7g; Cholesterol 0mg; Sodium 70mg; Carbohydrate 51g (Dietary Fiber 4g); Protein 2g

178

Raspberry-Peach Cobbler

6 servings

1/4 cup (1/2 stick) margarine

2/3 cup all-purpose flour

1/3 cup old-fashioned oats

1/2 cup granulated sugar

2 teaspoons baking powder

1/2 cup skim milk

1 teaspoon vanilla

2 cups sliced peeled peaches
    (2 to 3 medium)

1 1/2 cups fresh or unthawed
    frozen raspberries

1/4 cup granulated sugar

Powdered sugar, if desired

1. Heat oven to 350°. Melt margarine in square baking dish, 8 × 8 × 2 inches, in oven. Mix flour, oats, 1/2 cup granulated sugar and the baking powder in medium bowl. Stir in milk and vanilla just until moistened. Spoon batter evenly over margarine in dish (do not stir).

2. Mix peaches, raspberries and 1/4 cup granulated sugar. Spoon over batter (do not stir). Bake 35 to 40 minutes or until fruit is bubbly and crust is golden brown. Dust with powdered sugar.

1 Serving: Calories 275; Fat 8g; Cholesterol 0mg; Sodium 230mg; Carbohydrate 50g (Dietary Fiber 2g); Protein 2g

Cookie Dunkers

4 servings

1/2 cup chocolate fudge ice-cream topping, *heat if desired*

1/2 cup butterscotch or caramel ice-cream topping, *heat if desired*

1/2 cup frozen (thawed) whipped topping

12 cookies, any flavor (about 2 1/2 inches in diameter)

1. Place the ice-cream toppings and the whipped topping in separate small shallow bowls.

2. Dip cookies into ice-cream topping, then into whipped topping.

1 Serving: Calories 390; Fat 12g; Cholesterol 5mg; Sodium 260mg; Carbohydrate 67g (Dietary Fiber 1g); Protein 4g

Index

Metric Conversion Guide

Volume

U.S. Units	Canadian Metric	Australian Metric
1/4 teaspoon	1 mL	1 ml
1/2 teaspoon	2 mL	2 ml
1 teaspoon	5 mL	5 ml
1 tablespoon	15 mL	20 ml
1/4 cup	50 mL	60 ml
1/3 cup	75 mL	80 ml
1/2 cup	125 mL	125 ml
2/3 cup	150 mL	170 ml
3/4 cup	175 mL	190 ml
1 cup	250 mL	250 ml
1 quart	1 liter	1 liter
1 1/2 quarts	1.5 liters	1.5 liters
2 quarts	2 liters	2 liters
2 1/2 quarts	2.5 liters	2.5 liters
3 quarts	3 liters	3 liters
4 quarts	4 liters	4 liters

Weight

U.S. Units	Canadian Metric	Australian Metric
1 ounce	30 grams	30 grams
2 ounces	55 grams	60 grams
3 ounces	85 grams	90 grams
4 ounces (1/4 pound)	115 grams	125 grams
8 ounces (1/2 pound)	225 grams	225 grams
16 ounces (1 pound)	455 grams	500 grams
1 pound	455 grams	1/2 kilogram

Note: The recipes in this cookbook have not been developed or tested using metric measures. When converting recipes to metric, some variations in quality may be noted.

Measurements

Inches	Centimeters
1	2.5
2	5.0
3	7.5
4	10.0
5	12.5
6	15.0
7	17.5
8	20.5
9	23.0
10	25.5
11	28.0
12	30.5
13	33.0

Temperatures

Fahrenheit	Celsius
32°	0°
212°	100°
250°	120°
275°	140°
300°	150°
325°	160°
350°	180°
375°	190°
400°	200°
425°	220°
450°	230°
475°	240°
500°	260°

Equipment Used in Recipe Testing

We use equipment for testing that the majority of consumers use in their homes. If a specific piece of equipment (such as a wire whisk) is necessary for recipe success, it will be listed in the recipe.

- Cookware and bakeware without nonstick coatings were used, unless otherwise indicated.
- No dark colored, black or insulated bakeware was used.
- When a baking pan is specified in a recipe, a metal pan was used; a baking dish or pie plate means oven-proof glass was used.
- An electric hand mixer was used for mixing only when mixer speeds are specified in the recipe directions. When a mixer speed is not given, a spoon or fork was used.

Cooking Terms Glossary

Beat: Mix ingredients vigorously with spoon, fork, wire whisk, hand beater or electric mixer until smooth and uniform.

Boil: Heat liquid until bubbles rise continuously and break on the surface and steam is given off. For rolling boil, the bubbles form rapidly.

Chop: Cut into coarse or fine irregular pieces with a knife, food chopper, blender or food processor.

Cube: Cut into squares 1/2 inch or larger.

Dice: Cut into squares smaller than 1/2 inch.

Grate: Cut into tiny particles using small rough holes of grater (citrus peel or chocolate).

Grease: Rub the inside surface of a pan with shortening, using pastry brush, piece of waxed paper or paper towel, to prevent food from sticking during baking (as for some casseroles).

Julienne: Cut into thin, match-like strips, using knife or food processor (vegetables, fruits, meats).

Mix: Combine ingredients in any way that distributes them evenly.

Sauté: Cook foods in hot oil or margarine over medium-high heat with frequent tossing and turning motion.

Shred: Cut into long thin pieces by rubbing food across the holes of a shredder, as for cheese, or by using a knife to slice very thinly, as for cabbage.

Simmer: Cook in liquid just below the boiling point on top of the stove; usually after reducing heat from a boil. Bubbles will rise slowly and break just below the surface.

Stir: Mix ingredients until uniform consistency. Stir once in a while for stirring occasionally, often for stirring frequently and continuously for stirring constantly.

Toss: Tumble ingredients lightly with a lifting motion (such as green salad), usually to coat evenly or mix with another food.

Helpful Nutrition and Cooking Information

Nutrition Guidelines

We provide nutrition information for each recipe that includes calories, fat, cholesterol, sodium, carbohydrate, fiber and protein. Individual food choices can be based on this information

Recommended intake for a daily diet of 2,000 calories as set by the Food and Drug Administration:

Total Fat	Less than 65g
Saturated Fat	Less than 20g
Cholesterol	Less than 300mg
Sodium	Less than 2,400mg
Total Carbohydrate	300g
Dietary Fiber	25g

Criteria Used for Calculating Nutrition Information

- The first ingredient was used wherever a choice is given (such as 1/3 cup sour cream or plain yogurt).
- The first ingredient amount was used wherever a range is given (such as 3 to 3 1/2 pound cut-up broiler-fryer chicken).
- The first serving number was used wherever a range is given (such as 4 to 6 servings).
- "If desired" ingredients (such as sprinkle with brown sugar if desired) and recipe variations were not included .
- Only the amount of a marinade or frying oil that is estimated to be absorbed by the food during preparation or cooking was calculated.

Ingredients Used in Recipe Testing and Nutrition Calculations

- Ingredients used for testing represent those that the majority of consumers use in their homes: large eggs, 2% milk, 80% lean ground beef, canned ready-to-use chicken broth, and vegetable oil spread containing not less than 65% fat.
- Fat-free, low-fat or low-sodium products are not used, unless otherwise indicated.
- Solid vegetable shortening (not butter, margarine, nonstick cooking sprays or vegetable oil spread as they can cause sticking problems) is used to grease pans, unless otherwise indicated.

Sugar Cookie Tarts

4 servings

1/2 cup soft cream cheese with
strawberries or pineapple

4 round sugar cookies (4 inches
in diameter)

Desired toppings (sliced fresh
fruit, miniature chocolate
chips, chopped pecans, toasted
sliced almonds or jam)

1. Spread about 2 teaspoons cream cheese over each cookie. Arrange desired toppings above on cream cheese.

2. Serve immediately. Refrigerate any remaining cookies.

1 Serving: Calories 250; Fat 16g; Cholesterol 25mg; Sodium 170mg; Carbohydrate 25g (Dietary Fiber 1g); Protein 3g

182